BORROWED
OFFENSES

BORROWED OFFENSES

SATAN'S #1 WEAPON

BY VIC PORTER
FOREWORD BY BOB YANDIAN

Tate Publishing & Enterprises

This title is also available as a Tate Out Loud product. Visit www.tatepublishing.com for more information.

Scripture quotations marked "KJV" are taken from the Holy Bible, King James Version, Cambridge, 1769. Used by permission. All rights reserved.

Scripture quotations marked "NIV" are taken from the *Holy Bible, New International Version* ®, Copyright © 1973, 1978, 1984 by International Bible Society. Used by permission of Zondervan Publishing House. All rights reserved.

Scripture quotations marked "Msg" are taken from *The Message*, Copyright © 1993, 1994, 1995, 1996, 2000, 2001, 2002. Used by permission of NavPress Publishing Group. All rights reserved.

Scripture quotations marked "TLB" are taken from The Living Bible / Kenneth N. Taylor: Tyndale House, © Copyright 1997, 1971 by Tyndale House Publishers, Inc. Used by permission. All rights reserved.

Scripture quotations marked "TAB" are taken from The Amplified Bible, Old Testament, Copyright © 1965, 1987 by the Zondervan Corporation and The Amplified New Testament, Copyright © 1958, 1987 by The Lockman Foundation. Used by permission. All rights reserved.

The opinions expressed by the author are not necessarily those of Tate Publishing, LLC.

Published by Tate Publishing & Enterprises, LLC
127 E. Trade Center Terrace | Mustang, Oklahoma 73064 USA
1.888.361.9473 | www.tatepublishing.com

Tate Publishing is committed to excellence in the publishing industry. The company reflects the philosophy established by the founders, based on Psalm 68:11,
"The Lord gave the word and great was the company of those who published it."

Published in the United States of America

ISBN: 978-1-60462-915-6
1. Christian Relationships-Autobiography   2. Biblical Studies
First Printing June 1999
Second Printing February 2000
Third Printing October 2000
Fourth Printing March 2002
Fifth Printing May 2004
08.05.27

DEDICATION

R.L. and Rozena Zybach

True friends are rare. Thank you for
being a valuable part of our lives.

ACKNOWLEDGEMENTS

Special thanks to Col Stringer in Queensland, Australia for his permission to use his article entitled *"Get Your Hand Out of the Cage, Monkey."*

TABLE OF CONTENTS

FOREWORD

I have known Vic Porter for many years as a pastor and a personal friend.

This book he has written comes straight from his personal experience and should strike a chord in your heart.

I know it did mine. I found this book so good, I immediately taught it to my congregation.

Don't buy this book and leave it on the shelf. Read it and watch your life change directions.

Bob Yandian

INTRODUCTION

As a pastor and teacher, my desire for the people is to always teach them how to live more successful lives. It is my purpose, in these pages, to teach by the Word and by my personal experience the importance of refusing to embrace any and all offenses.

Often we think that leaders are exempt from problems; that they never have any difficulty and their lives go smoothly. That is simply not true. Such has been the case with our lives, and so *Borrowed Offenses* has been written.

I have lived every page of this book. It's more than words on a page. Every word, every paragraph, every chapter is filled with emotion and the desire to minister truth to the Body of Christ. I can honestly say, in the content of each word, there is no anger.

We all have been offended at one time or another. Some people have learned to turn loose of the offense.

Unfortunately, some have embraced the offense and have lived their lives being controlled by the plan of the enemy.

An offense is a seed that the devil can use against you to get you to oppose yourself. If the devil can get you to oppose yourself, he begins to control your life.

One thing I have found worse than a direct offense is a borrowed offense. A borrowed offense is someone else's offense. It has nothing to do with you. You take another person's offense and make it yours.

That is what I did. I took another person's offense and made it mine. He became offended and told me about it. To my regret, I took his offense. I can tell you, you do not want to do that. I wish I had read this book before I borrowed my friend's offense. It would have saved me a lot of heartache.

Please read this book with an open heart. Be brave enough to allow the Holy Spirit to examine your heart to see if you have embraced any offenses. If you have, release them and enjoy your freedom in Jesus Christ.

Blessings!
Vic Porter

THE NATURE OF AN OFFENSE

A few years ago in a town near where we lived, some people were going to put up a building for a new business. They needed a lot of fill dirt for the foundation so they brought in many truckloads of dirt, spread it out, and then let it settle for a while. After it had settled, the engineer signed his name signifying that it was safe to build on this property.

It was a retail business with a lot of traffic and after about four years the building began to crack. Obviously, there was a foundational problem, and the engineer who signed his name had to go back and reconstruct the building from underneath and secure it.

A Strong Foundation of the Word

That is the way a lot of believers' lives are. They think they can handle the things in their lives, but the ground is not ready yet, and so they begin to build on sand. Anytime you build on sand; the wind, the waves, or other forces eventually will crack the foundation. You can get through life with a cracked foundation, but you are not going to enjoy it as much as you could. You need to build a strong foundation of the Word to keep the pressures of the world from destroying you.

> The sower soweth the word. And these are they by the wayside, where the word is sown; but when they have heard, Satan cometh immediately, and taketh away the word that was sown in their hearts. And these are they likewise which are sown on stony ground; who, when they have heard the word, immediately receive it with gladness; And have no root in themselves, and so endure but for a time: afterward, when affliction or persecution ariseth for the word's sake, immediately they are offended. And these are they which are sown among thorns; such as hear the word, And the cares of this world, and the deceitfulness of riches, and the lusts of other things entering in, choke the word, and it becometh unfruitful. And these are they which are sown on good ground; such as hear the word, and receive it, and bring forth fruit, some thirtyfold, some sixty, and some a hundred.
>
> Mark 4:14–20 (KJV)

You need to strive to become the good ground mentioned in verse 20. Verse 20 needs to be your goal in life so when offenses or problems come, they will not affect you or push you down. Your whole life should be grounded upon the Word of God, the rock of the Lord Jesus Christ, and not upon the sand. Anything that is built upon the sand is going to crumble.

In verse 17, it says, "immediately they are offended." One of the biggest hindrances in doing the will of God is that people become offended.

Tom Underhill, a pastor friend of mine said, *"If you can be offended, then you will be."*

You are going to have the opportunity to be offended. The devil will make sure of it. One of his jobs is to make sure you get offended, if you can be.

Types of Offenses

Sometimes we become offended and then we offend. Offenses are designed by the enemy to keep the message of the Word from operating in our lives. When we become offended, we allow those offenses to stop the flow of the kingdom of God in our lives.

There are three types of offenses. The first is a *direct offense*. The second type of offense is *one that is given*. The third type of offense is *one that is borrowed*.

A *direct offense* is something that happened directly to you. We all have had direct offenses. How do you respond? It hurts, does it not?

Then there are *given offenses*. We all know people with a broken heart. We know there has been a cause for their broken heart. What we fail to realize is that there are times when we have been the offender of the one who is broken hearted. We need to be sensitive to the things we have done to offend and cause broken hearts. In some situations we have become the offenders.

You may offend someone on purpose, knowing exactly

what you are doing, or you may offend someone without realizing it. We probably do not want to say yes as quickly to offending on purpose as we would to offending accidentally.

As you are reading this book, and you look back to situations of your life, have you been the culprit offending someone? I know I have. Have you ever been misunderstood and the misunderstanding caused an offense?

Borrowed Offenses

The third type of offense is a *borrowed offense*. Borrowing an offense is a choice you do not have to make. When you borrow an offense from someone, you are not helping them by sharing the offense. You are stopping the Kingdom of God from operating in you. You are hurting you. You are clogging up your life.

So what is a borrowed offense? Simply this: someone was offended and it had nothing to do with you, but you made a choice to take it anyway. Have you ever borrowed an offense before? A borrowed offense is the most damaging of all, besides being the most stupid. Do you know why? It had nothing to do with you. Satan knows exactly who will borrow an offense. Some people will pick up an offense automatically.

Be a Peacemaker

Suppose someone came up to you and said you were not doing a very good job at work; that is a direct offense. If you were the one saying it, then you would be giving an offense, but if your friend told you someone had said that to her and you decided not to ever speak to that person again, that would be a borrowed offense.

Why am I teaching this? I borrowed an offense. It will eat your lunch! It did mine. You may think you know who was right, but if you were not there you can not possibly know. If you were there, you are supposed to be a peacemaker, not an offense supporter. Do not ever let someone else's hurts become yours. If you love your friend, speak peace, not hate, into the situation.

The offense I borrowed had nothing to do with me, but as I borrowed it, it became real to me, and it began to affect my thinking. My wife often used the phrase "borrowed offense" to help me see what was happening and to encourage me to let go of it.

Where Offenses Come From

Where do offenses come from? Offenses come from people, Christians or non-Christians who do not know who they are in Christ. If we know who we are, then we know that Jesus took our offenses on himself, and paid the price to set us free from them.

There are two sets of plans available to us for our lives. God has one, and the enemy, Satan, has one. When we borrow someone else's offenses and hold on to them, it limits our ability to see the plan, purpose, and direction of God for our lives.

When our vision is blocked by offenses, we fail to see where we are going. When we cannot see where we are going, we run into Satan's plans for us.

When I borrowed that offense, my wife kept saying, "You are just letting that eat at you, and it is not even yours." It is one thing to let a direct offense chew you up, but it is really stupid to let a borrowed offense chew you up and destroy you.

When you take an offense and hold onto it, it becomes your security. If someone comes along and teaches a message like this and asks you to give up your offense, is your response, "No, I am going to fight for this. I am going to bed with it every night. This is just like my blanket. I'm going to hold on to it!"

You are on your way to developing a grudge. You want to hold on to your grudge because it has become your security. What would you do if you did not have it?

We deal with life in either the Spirit realm or the natural realm. We are spirit beings in a natural body. In the natural you might say, "Well I have a right to keep it. You should have heard what happened. You would understand if you knew what happened."

If you are operating in the natural, which many people do, it is normal to take, hold onto, or borrow an offense. Whenever you take on or borrow an offense, do you know what you are going to end up doing?

You are going to end up being a giver of offenses. 1 Timothy 5:13 (KJV) states, "And withal they learn to be idle, wandering about from house to house; and not only idle, but tattlers also and busybodies, speaking things which they ought not."

Also 1 Peter 4:15 (KJV) tells us "But let none of you suffer as a murderer, or as a thief, or as an evildoer, or as a busybody in other men's matters." Isn't it interesting that the Spirit of God placed a "busybody in other men's matters," along with a thief and a murderer and an evildoer? He said, "let none of you suffer as ... " Do busybodies suffer? Yes, they do. Do you know why they suffer?

They suffer because they have taken an offense and now have begun to give them out. He said, "... in another man's matter" or, in another man's business. You know what is your business. You know when someone else's business isn't yours.

> And that ye study to be quiet, and to do your own business, and to work with your own hands, as we commanded you; That ye may walk honestly toward them that are without, and that ye may have lack of nothing.
>
> 1 Thessalonians 4:11, 12 (KJV)

Sometimes people fail to see who they are or can be in Christ. When they cannot see who they are, they begin to take or borrow offenses, and begin to get into other people's business. Then they can think they know everything. They go from place to place trying to find out about other people's business so they can be an authority.

We need to see others the way that God sees them. They are the righteousness of God in Christ Jesus. When others get down, we need to recognize it, be understanding, and encourage them—not join sides with them.

If they took an offense, and I do not know who I am in Christ, I might take that offense with them. Now there are two in agreement. You know what happens when you get two in agreement about an offense? Both fail to see the plan, purpose and direction of God for their lives.

You might ask, "Well, what is the plan, purpose and

direction of God?" You are. You are a complex person that God has plans, purposes, and direction for.

You have things going on in your head and in your heart. You hurt from time to time, and God, through revelation knowledge of His Word wants to minister to you and set you free in those areas.

When you apply the truth of His Word in your life, you will be able to know and carry out His purposes. He has to have you free before you can minister to other people.

A Root of Bitterness

Why does the devil try to use offenses? Look at Hebrews 12:15, "Looking diligently lest any man fail of the grace of God; lest any root of bitterness springing up trouble you, and thereby many be defiled."

When the root of bitterness springs up inside of us, it troubles us, and when we are troubled, we trouble other people.

When people are spitting out venom toward you, or toward someone else, look beyond what they are doing and see their real need. Their real need is to be loved, to be ministered to, and set free from the hurt inside them.

Whenever venom is spewed out into the church world, or into the business world, offenses are taken. This causes the root of bitterness to be planted in the heart, and the product of bitterness is wrath.

Anytime we, or those around us, are constantly running someone else down, it is not because that other person is so bad, but because we are hurt. The only reason we do that is because of the seed of the root of bitterness that is there. The root of bitterness has produced wrath.

If someone has been offended, and he takes the offense, the devil thinks to himself, "Now I have him. He has taken that offense. He has willfully taken it. Therefore, I can cause the seed of bitterness to be rooted in his heart. Then the things that come out of his mouth will be wrath."

I am not just talking about one particular person. I am talking about me, you, people down the block, people up the block, people right across the street from where you are.

People are Important

So, why is this important? It is important because we are dealing with people. We are dealing with the very reason that Jesus Christ died.

Proverbs 29:18 (KJV) says, "Where there is no vision, the people perish." I believe we have to have a vision. I have one. Do you know what's happening to my vision? It is changing in its "busyness." I have had to lay down that "busy, reach the goal" part of my vision and pick up what is important.

People are important. Your church may need a building, but reaching the goal of a building is less important than people are.

The purpose of the body of Christ is to reach down on the inside of people who cannot lift their hands, and minister life to them so they can lift up their hands and rejoice.

Look at Hebrews 12:15 (KJV) again, "Looking diligently lest any man fail of the grace of God; lest any root of bitterness springing up trouble you..."

The root of bitterness is going to trouble you first. When you are troubled, you can only give what you have and you are going to trouble other people.

You might ask, "What do you mean by troubling other people?" I mean, creating offenses so that people will take them. When you and I create offenses and people take them, or we borrow offenses, we have failed to see the purpose of the church.

The purpose of the church is not a building, it is not a bus, it is not this or that—it is *you*! You are the reason Jesus died. That other person is the reason that Jesus died.

Do you know the song, "He looked beyond my fault and saw my need"? Aren't you glad He did?

If He looked beyond your faults and saw your need, don't you realize there are people who wish you would look beyond their faults and see their need? If your vision is clouded by offenses, you cannot see their need.

Offenses lead to a root of bitterness. The root of bitterness produces unforgiveness. I know we don't like to hear this; however, unforgiveness produces hatred that, if left unchecked, has no limit to its destructive ability.

Have you ever had dandelions in your yard? You mowed them down yesterday, and today they are back! Do you know how to avoid having dandelions back tomorrow? Dig up the roots!

If we take on an offense, we can be establishing the root of bitterness in our heart and unforgiveness will follow. If we have allowed things to go this far, can we believe God for our finances?

Give me a break! In taking an offense we are spending our life not depositing our life into others.

A Conversation of Wrath

"I do not know why all my needs are not met—I have given and given!" We cannot expect our needs to be met when there is unforgiveness in our hearts.

How do you know if you have a root of bitterness?

Go with me to Ephesians 4: 31–32 (KJV), "Let all bitterness, and wrath, and anger, and clamor, and evil speaking be put away from you, with all malice. And be ye kind one to another, tenderhearted, forgiving one another, even as God for Christ's sake has forgiven you."

How do you know whether you have a root of bitterness or not? Listen to what is coming out of your mouth. Is evil speaking coming out of you? The root of bitterness produces a conversation of wrath.

BORROWED OFFENSES

The third type of offense is a *borrowed offense*. A borrowed offense is when someone does something wrong to someone you know, but it does not involve you. Then they tell you how they were treated and you get angry for them. You have just taken their offense. That is a borrowed offense. It had nothing to do with you, but all of a sudden it becomes a very active part of your life and your conversation.

An Act of Stupidity

So you begin to take on someone else's problems, someone else's offenses, and someone else's situation. You literally take it and embrace it—it becomes a part of you. You go around telling people exactly what happened. Maybe you were there. Maybe you did see what happened, but maybe you do not know everything else about it! Is that possible? Even if you did know everything else, you do not need to borrow someone else's offense.

Borrowing an offense from someone else is stupid because it tears you up, and it does not help the other person. If you choose to borrow someone else's offense, you are tying up the kingdom of God from operating in your life. An offense stops the kingdom of God from operating not only in your own life, but also in the lives of other people.

Now, we said that an offense produces a root of bitterness which produces unforgiveness. I would venture to say that everyone would walk in total forgiveness if there were never any offenses.

A Trick of the Enemy

The enemy wants offenses to take place so that some people will grab hold of them and nurture them. Then they become a root of bitterness, and that root of bitterness will cause unforgiveness to take place in a man's heart. We fail to forgive others. "For with the same measure that ye mete withal it shall be measured to you again." (Luke 6:38, KJV)

What happens when we as part of the body of Christ take an offense, allow it to become a root of bitterness, and produce unforgiveness? If you cannot or will not forgive, others may not forgive you. We do not want to face the Lord with unforgiveness in our hearts.

I want to encourage you, if you have unforgiveness or a root of bitterness toward anyone, change your heart and begin to deal with it. If you do not, you are not holding it over them—you are holding it over yourself! You are not hurting them—you are only hurting yourself.

I could interview everyone who reads this book, and we could get all kinds of stories of how different people have been offended. Those offenses are a trick of the enemy. It is a spiritual principle that happens. Whenever an offense comes, it releases something in the spirit realm that stops the kingdom of God from operating in your life. You do not want to mess with offenses. Forget them.

If you are sitting there right now and you are offended, read very carefully the things I am going to say. You need to get rid of it. You are ending your effectiveness in the kingdom of God if you do not.

Free to Receive

> Then said Jesus to them again, Peace be unto you: as my Father hath sent me, even so send I you. And when he had said this, he breathed on them, and saith unto them. Receive ye the Holy Ghost: Whose soever sins ye remit [forgive], they are remitted unto them; and whose soever sins ye retain, [do not forgive], they are retained.
>
> John 20:21–23 (KJV)

Jesus came to them and said, "Receive ye the Holy Ghost," or receive the infilling of the power of the Spirit of God. The purpose of the infilling of the Holy Spirit is so that you will become a witness on the earth.

Jesus said in John 20:23 (KJV), "Whose soever sins ye

remit, they are remitted unto them; and whose soever sins ye retain, they are retained."

"If you forgive anyone his sins, they are forgiven…" (John 20:23, NIV). Now read the rest of the verse, "…if you do not forgive them, they are not forgiven." If you will not forgive, those sins are retained, and they will attach themselves to you. Retaining a sin or unforgiveness is taking the offense and making it yours.

Have you ever said, "I will never do what my parents did to me?" Those are famous last words. If you do not forgive them, you will do exactly what they did. Do you know why? It is because you retained it and it became a part of you. You were offended and never let it go.

In Numbers 14:18 (KJV), it says the sins of the fathers are passed down to the third and fourth generation. I wonder why that is. Could it be because of unforgiveness?

Turn Loose of Them!

You do not want to retain the sins of your father or your mother. You may be sitting there right now, married for 25–30 years, and still retaining or holding onto, through unforgiveness, certain things your parent may or may not have done in your childhood. Forgive and turn loose of them! The longer you hold on to these things the more they become a part of you. You are embracing the things they did that may not have been right. For example, I started school when I was too young simply because this was convenient for my parents. I was the youngest in my class so I had to pretend I was more mature than I was. I tried hard to be "cool" to make up for my immaturity. Because of this I always felt I never measured up. I felt my life would have been better if I had been allowed to wait until I was a more appropriate age to begin school. Now I realize my parents didn't have other options in our small rural community at that time and they didn't realize how this would affect me. I had to turn loose of it.

I will tell you another thing I dealt with in the past. As a young boy I knew about salvation. I had considered it for years. I went to church camp, raised my hand, and wanted to get saved, but I didn't go up front and receive Jesus as my Savior for many years. It haunted me for a long time.

Once I got saved I realized, "This is what I needed to do all along." I needed to get it done. I had been running around there for 6 or 8 years knowing I needed to get saved, but refusing to do it. Finally, I did it.

At that time, I was in a denominational church. About four years later, I found out about the power of the Holy Spirit. No one in my denomination had told me about it. "Why didn't they tell me about this power?"

They did not tell me because they did not know. At least some of them did not know. For a period of time I was offended. "You didn't tell me I could be totally set free. You didn't tell me that there was power."

If I had retained that and gotten mad at that denomination, or gotten mad at a person because they failed to tell me something that would set me free, I might never have received it.

I am responsible for my life. I had to forgive them and go on. They were only responsible for what they knew. I have a responsibility to share with you the principles of the truth that I know to the best of my ability.

Whether you live it or do not live it is not my responsibility—it is yours. Whether I live it or whether I do not live it is not your responsibility—it is mine.

Being Sensitive to Hear God's Voice

Do you know how missionaries get sent into different areas of the world? There is someone in a remote area seeking to know the truth about God. They look at the earth, the heavens, and the stars and they ask, "Is there a God? If there is a God, please send someone our way to tell us about Him!" The Spirit of God hears that and drops it into someone's heart 5,000 miles away who is willing to obey God. The Spirit of God sends that person to that faraway place so those people who are spiritually hungry may receive the Lord Jesus Christ.

Those people want to know the truth. God wants to work through you and me by the power of the Spirit of God in such a manner that we would be so sensitive that we hear His still, small voice down inside of us at any time and obey.

If we take on offenses, we will not hear Him. When you take an offense, you are putting earplugs in your spiritual ears. Then the still, small voice is so still and so small that you do not hear or pay attention to what is happening.

Now look at John 20:23 (KJV) again, "whose soever sins ye remit, they are remitted unto them; and whose soever sins ye retain, they are retained." Turn loose of them. They matter in the realm of the Spirit because they will tie up the flow of God in your life.

Realities of the Spirit Realm

> And he said, So is the kingdom of God, as if a man should cast seed into the ground; And should sleep, and rise night and day, and the seed should spring and grow up, he knoweth not how. For the earth bringeth forth fruit of herself; first the blade, then the ear, after that the full corn in the ear. But when the fruit is brought forth, immediately he putteth in the sickle, because the harvest is come.
>
> Mark 4:26–29 (KJV)

In Mark 4:26–29 (KJV), Jesus talks about the principle of sowing and reaping. He explains that you place a grain of corn in the ground and it grows up and becomes a stalk, then becomes a full ear of corn, and then the harvest comes.

Jesus is simply saying here that this is the very same way that the kingdom of God, or the spirit realm operates. The spirit realm is more real than the natural realm. The things that are in the spirit realm created everything you see and touch in the natural realm.

We think, "Oh, we're just talking. Talk doesn't mean anything." Your words are going into the realm of the spirit! You may not be able to see them, touch them, or feel them, but your words are affecting the activity of the spirit realm. Your words carry a lot of power and authority, and they affect things in the spirit realm.

Jesus said, "the words that I speak unto you, they are spirit and they are life" (John 6: 63, KJV). His words are spirit and life. Our words are also spirit, and release either life or death.

Your words released out of your mouth affect the spirit realm. They affect what the angels can do for you. They affect what the devil can do. They affect your life. We think, "Oh, my words are not important." But they ARE important! Your words affect your whole life!

What happens when we are caught up in an offense and we begin to give that offense back out? We are affecting the lives of other people!

Turn Loose of It!

A few years ago I had a phone call that was not directed at me personally. It was a problem with another situation in another ministry. It made me so mad!

Listen to me carefully. That phone call was so devastating to me that I borrowed it and carried it with me for about a year and a half. I would like to tell you it did not faze me one bit! But I will tell you this. I believe, in the name of Jesus, that if I get another phone call like that, it will not faze me.

Do not ever be that stupid. Turn loose of it. Do not carry anything that long because it will affect you! Are you hearing me? Do not retain any of these things. Turn loose of them.

Why does Proverbs 4:20, 23 (KJV) tell us, "attend to my Words...Keep thy heart with all diligence"? Why does the writer of Hebrews caution us to be, "looking diligently," at our lives? (Hebrews 12:15, KJV)?

God is trying to tell us to pay attention to the things that are being said around you, and if there are offenses out there (and there are), refuse them. You do not want them. It is like a disease that will eat you up.

Do you think you would really enjoy having cancer? No, you would not enjoy that, and you also would not enjoy the effects of a borrowed offense. It is worse than cancer. It will destroy your life and the things of God in your life.

A Root of Bitterness

Do you know whether or not you have a root of bitterness in your life? None of us really want a root of bitterness in our life.

When you take an offense, the next step is bitterness. The root of bitterness will set in, and if you continue to nurture it, unforgiveness develops in your heart. When unforgiveness develops you begin to retain the sins you won't forgive. The very thing you are retaining will direct your life. Your life is directed by how you deal with offenses.

> Let all bitterness, and wrath, and anger, and clamor, and evil speaking, be put away from you, with all malice: And be ye kind one to another, tenderhearted, forgiving one another, even as God for Christ's sake hath forgiven you.
>
> Ephesians 4: 31, 32 (KJV)

Bitterness, or a root of bitterness, in your heart has fruit to it. That fruit is the wrath that comes out of your mouth. You can tell whether a root of bitterness is there by how you react and by the words that come out of your mouth toward someone else.

Has someone ever offended you and you did not want to ever see that person again? Perhaps you think, "Maybe it will all go away if I never see them again."

All of a sudden they show up, or you see them in a store. You may think to yourself, "Oh, I won't speak to them because they offended me." But in essence, you are still trying to collect that debt that you think they owe you.

It is not how much Word you can confess that makes you spiritual. It is how much Word you let affect your life that makes you spiritual.

You are not here just to be blessed—you are here to bless people. We often think, "I do not have a problem. I have forgiven them. I have turned loose of them."

What determines whether you have turned loose of that person, released them and forgiven them? It is when you have nothing but love and compassion for them when you see them, instead of, "Some day you'll get it! Watch your back."

Do you know what God would do? What would Jesus do in a situation like that? He'd make sure that every need they had was met!

You and I need to come to the place in our lives that when we see people who have done us wrong, or people we have done wrong, it does not affect us.

Have you ever thought, "I'll forgive you, but I won't forget it." What you are actually saying is, "I'm forgiving you, but I'm really not. Next time I see you, I'll remember and I'll get mad all over again."

Jesus is Our Substitute

Do you know what true freedom is? Listen to me carefully. True freedom is your ability to live your life successfully with no desire to collect any debt that anyone owes you. Get to the place where nothing affects you and you are free. I long for that freedom and you should too.

2 Corinthians 5:21 (KJV) tells us, "For He hath made him to be sin for us, who knew no sin, that we might be made the righteousness of God in him." When you take an offense you are saying, "Jesus became my substitute in the punishment of sin, in sickness and disease, in poverty, but not in this offense."

On the cross Jesus became the complete substitute for everything you will ever go through in life. On the cross Jesus was saying, "Blame me, release them." He paid the price for your sins as well as the sins of those who offend you.

Stephen's last words when he was being stoned were, "Lord, don't charge them with this sin!" (Acts 7:60, TLB). That is a tough thing for any man to say. Jesus stood up when Stephen said that. Would you want Jesus to stand up because of you? Turn loose of every offense that you have kept.

Unforgiveness has the power to control your life. Jesus became our substitute for sickness and disease. He became our substitute for poverty. He even became our substitute for spiritual death. Jesus became our substitute for confusion. Jesus became our substitute for every area in our life. If He became our true substitute, then He became our complete substitute.

Jesus became the substitute for every offense that has ever come your way. You and I need to realize and understand, "Hey, He became my substitute for that offense. Therefore, I don't have to take it." He became your substitute in every sense, and it literally means you can walk in total freedom in your every day life.

Sometimes we say, "Well, yeah, He became our substitute,

I receive that part of it, but I'm not going to turn loose of this!" However, you can be free by allowing Jesus to become the substitute for every offense that has ever come to you.

"Get your Hand out of the Cage, Monkey!"

In March of 1994, I read an article by Col Stringer entitled "GET YOUR HAND OUT OfTHE CAGE, MONKEY!" He was watching a documentary on African monkeys and how people were capturing and killing them. This is what he said:

> "GET YOUR HAND OUT OF THE CAGE, MONKEY!" I almost shouted those words out loud recently. And when I did, the Spirit of God revealed something to me I'll never forget.
>
> At the time, I had just seen a documentary that portrayed how African monkeys are captured and killed. I had watched in amazement as the natives set out a series of cages, each one equipped with a bait stick.
>
> The bait stick, which might be a bright object, a piece of food, or anything else that the monkey might want, served to lure the monkeys to the cages. Too smart to actually go inside the cages, however, the monkeys would simply reach through the bars and grab the bait stick.
>
> The problem was this, since the stick was too large to get through the bars, the only way the monkey could get his hand back out of the cage, was to drop it. Dropping the stick is the one thing that monkeys absolutely refuse to do.
>
> They would roll, kick and squeal. They would bare their teeth. They would do everything but let go of the stick.
>
> Even when the natives came out and began to

bash them over the head, they wouldn't let go. It was a startling sight. Yet even more startling, was the question the Holy Spirit asked me some time later, after I'd heard Pastor Phil Goudeaux speaking on the subject, '*How many monkeys do you know in the church?*'

I knew exactly what he meant. He was telling me that the very same thing that happened to those monkeys is happening to the Church today.

Just like the natives he knows we're too smart to go into his cage. So he put in a bait stick.

Do you know what that bait stick is? I call it a *scandalon* because that's the Greek word used in the New Testament. But the English translation of it is *offense*.

The number one tactic the devil is using today to destroy the lives of believers is to get us offended.

It's true, there are multitudes of believers walking around with monumental chips on their shoulders. I travel all over the world teaching in various churches. And I can confidently say that if I went into any city, rounded up all the Christians who had dropped out of church because they had been offended in one way or another and put them all together in one church, it would be the largest church in town.

What's more, once they take offense, most believers will hold on to it at any price. Even when the devil is bashing them over the head, they refuse to let it go. I know that from experience because in times past, I have been one of them.

But recently that's changed. Since then I've begun to heed and obey the voice of God when He says to me, "*Get your hand out of the cage, Monkey!*"

Count the Cost

If you're anything like I was when the Lord first started dealing with me about offenses, you may not even realize that you have your hand in the cage. Most Christians don't. They rationalize and justify themselves by saying, "Well, after what that person did to me, I just can't help feeling this way."

That's what I did. Some time ago the Spirit of God said to me, "You are offended." And I said, "No Lord. I'm not offended. I'm just a little hurt."

"Then why do you get a knot in your stomach every time you see that person?" He asked. "Why does it bother you when you hear someone else praising him? I'll tell you why. You have your hand in the cage!"

Listen, if you have your hand in the cage today, admit it. If you don't, it could cost you your ministry. It could cost you your children. It could cost you your finances. It could even cost you your life.

Why? The Bible tells us that the devil uses offenses to steal the Word from our heart.

The author of this article goes on to quote Mark 4:15 (KJV), "…Satan cometh immediately, and taketh away the word that was sown in their hearts." The devil will steal the Word you have in your heart if you have taken offense and refuse to let go.

He tells about a pastor he had ministered with in a large church who, one day left his church, his family, everything. Later he spoke to him and asked him what was going on. He said, "I don't want to hear anything about God. I'm not interested. Just leave me alone." The cause was that he had been offended, and through the offenses the devil stole the Word from his heart.

The Word will not work in your life if you don't, "Get your hand out of the cage, Monkey!"

Affecting the Anointing

Let's look at how offenses affect the anointing. In Mark 6:2, Mark is talking about Jesus as He taught in the synagogue. Those that heard him were amazed at the wisdom He had and the miracles He wrought. They could not believe that a man, just a carpenter related to people they knew, could be saying and doing these things. He was just "one of them."

They got offended that He would presume to teach them. In Mark 6:5 (KJV), it says that because of their offense, "he could there do no mighty work, save that he laid his hands upon a few sick folk, and healed them."

In this situation, the anointing power of God was there to heal, but because the people had taken offense, Jesus could not heal them.

The author's question to all this was, "If Jesus couldn't get offended people healed, how do you think your pastor is going to be able to? Can you afford to cut yourself off from the anointing of God?"

"Get your hand out of the cage, monkey!" It is your choice and your decision. No one can do it for you. No one can do it for me.

I did not start studying about offenses to write this book. I studied the areas of offenses for myself. I wanted to see where

I was. I wanted to know where my heart was. I cannot tell you where your heart is. Only you can find that out for yourself.

Our relationships in life are so important that we do not need to spend our time with our hand in the cage. If you have the opportunity to have an offense, for your sake, for the body of Christ's sake, for your family's sake, for your employer's sake, for your employee's sake, have enough sense to turn loose of the offense.

We said earlier that there are many Christians out there trying to collect debts. Are you one of them?

Raising Children Free from Offenses

Three lifestyles that children are raised under are grace, law, or lawlessness. We raise children with one, or a blend of these three lifestyles. Whatever you put into a child is what they become. Whatever you receive as a person is what you become.

In a home where children are raised under the law, or a performance-based life is advocated, children learn that they must perform a certain way to get the love and approval of the parent. That becomes embedded in their soul. They will begin to respond to that and will even learn how to deceive their parents to try to gain the love and approval they need.

In a home of lawlessness there are no guidelines, and so they sense this means, "Go ahead and do what you want to and I will do what I want to." It disguises itself as love but it is not. Kids who are raised in a lawless lifestyle often end up spending time in jails or hospitals.

Children who are raised in a home of law often rebel at discipline. Children who were raised in a lawless home often wish they would have had some discipline. Law will use discipline as a form of punishment. In lawlessness there are no boundaries, so a child has no basis for making decisions. Pain is created in the atmosphere of a home governed by law or by lawlessness.

Then there is the home where children are raised under grace. Grace has standards, but the standards are the Word of God. Under grace, you find there is correction, but it is done because you love the child whether they perform well or not. Performance is not the issue. You love them if they perform well or if they don't.

These three have different standards. Grace has the standard of the Word, law has a standard of performance, and lawlessness has no standard at all. Whichever of these three you deposit into a child determines what that child is going to be. There may be times when we raise children with a little of all three.

We often wonder why we are so messed up in our thinking, and a lot of it has to do with the way we were trained. The way we were raised affects how we respond to the Word.

The Little Sins

There are two types of sins. There are inward sins and outward sins.

Proverbs 6: 16 talks about seven things that are an abomination to God. If you read through these, you will find there are three that are outward sins and the others are inward sins.

An outward sin would be fornication, getting drunk, or lying. We as Christians normally don't do these things, and we say, "You'll never find me guilty of those outward sins."

But in Song of Solomon 2: 15 (KJV) it says, "…the little foxes, that spoil the vines:" That is, we guard against the big things people can see, but cover the inward sins with a smile. It is the inward sins that destroy. The little things are the anger, bitterness, and hatred that don't show outwardly.

I John 1: 9 (KJV) tells us what to do in order to be free from any sins we may commit, "If we confess our sins, he is faithful and just to forgive us our sins, and to cleanse us from all unrighteousness."

CHAINED TO OFFENSES

We acted out a scenario in church one day so I could give the congregation a visual aid showing what offenses do to a person. This is what really happens in the realm of the spirit.

Who Is Your Buddy?

Picture in your mind a chain tied to your arm. The other end of the chain is attached to a demonic spirit. Now picture all these labels attached to the demonic spirit, such as jealousy, hatred, unforgiveness, sickness, disease, and poverty.

These are negative forces in the realm of the spirit, and they manifest in the natural realm. The demonic spirit uses these negative forces to get us into a situation where we are susceptible to the offenses he wants to tie us up with.

This demonstrates how a demonic spirit ties himself to you when you are in a situation of borrowing offenses. When we take on an offense, direct or borrowed, the demonic spirit can rightfully chain himself to us, and as long as we will stay in that offense, he will stay right there with us. We cannot send him away without dealing with the offense according to the principles of the Word.

The demonic spirit enjoys being around us. He will present many arguments to us as to why we should rightfully be offended. He will help us to avoid the Word. He will drag us back into dwelling on the offense and generally create an atmosphere of despair and sadness in our life.

This demonic spirit is a thief of joy. If he can steal your joy, he can rob you of your strength.

If you hear the Word on how to be set free, the demonic spirit will immediately remind you of how bad it really was. Mark 4:15 (KJV) says, "Satan cometh immediately and taketh away the word that was sown in their hearts."

If you speak the Word to your offense, the demonic spirit will beg and plead with you to be mad, be sad, or be spiteful. He wants you to be anything but full of the Word. If you remain strong and speak the Word, he will have to go. However, he will not miss you for he is on to his next victim.

Staying Out of Offenses

Keep this picture in mind if you are tempted to give in to an offense. The easiest way to take care of an offense is to never accept one to begin with.

It takes more energy to speak out cursing over people than it does to speak out blessing. The flesh will speak evil over people so easily. The Spirit of God inside of you doesn't want to do that. He wants to speak out blessing. The flesh wants to take on a spirit of death. By embracing an offense you attract poverty, confusion, sickness, and death to your life. The Spirit inside of you wants to take on the spirit of life.

Have you taken offense? Now let me ask you this. What are you going to do with it?

If you want to be free from an offense, say this, "Father, in the name of Jesus, I repent of any offense that I have ever taken, and I command it's power to be broken over my life. And Father, I receive your spirit of blessing over my life. In Jesus' name. Amen."

DEALING WITH OFFENSES

If we do not pay attention to the offenses coming and going in our lives, we may allow one to set up residence.

Again in Hebrews 12:15 (KJV), we want to look at another part of the verse, "Looking diligently lest any man fail of the grace of God; lest any root of bitterness springing up trouble you, and thereby many be defiled."

An offense, if not properly taken care of, will produce a root of bitterness in a person's life. So the root of bitterness comes from an offense you take.

We can be a giver of an offense because once we have taken an offense, we have the capacity to give it back out.

Hebrews 12:15 (KJV) says, "Looking diligently if any man fail of the grace of God; lest the root of bitterness ..."

The root of bitterness is produced because an offense has been taken. It is springing up to trouble you, and because it troubles you, you will trouble or defile many other people.

When you become offended and you do not deal with it according to the Word, the root of bitterness can try to sneak into your heart and begin to make its abode there. Then it springs up in you. When it springs up in you, it troubles you. When it troubles you, you are going to trouble someone else.

What is in your heart will come out. Have you troubled other people because of something that's happened to you? We all have done that. This is exactly what it is saying, "…thereby many be defiled." When you are troubled by offenses, you will trouble others.

Looking Diligently

Now remember the words, "looking diligently" while we look at some more verses for a moment.

> My son, attend to my words; incline thine ear to my sayings. Let them not depart from thine eyes; keep them in the midst of thine heart. For they are life to those who find them, and health to all their flesh. Keep thy heart with all diligence; for out of it are the issues of life. Put away from thee a froward mouth, and perverse lips put far from thee. Let thine eyes look right on, and let thine eyelids look straight before thee. Ponder the path of thy feet, and let all thy ways be established. Turn not to the right hand nor to the left: remove thy foot from evil.
>
> Proverbs 4:20–22 (KJV)

Hebrew 12:15 (KJV) says, "looking diligently…" Proverbs 4:20 says the same thing, "My son, attend to my words". Attend unto His words.

Proverbs 4:23 (KJV) says to, "keep your heart ... for out of it are the issues of life." You could say it this way, "for out of it flow the issues of life." Every issue of your life comes from your heart. What you put into your heart is what you are going to walk in.

If you retain an offense, it will spring up and trouble you, and when it springs up and troubles you, you are going to give it back out because that is all you have to give. If you retain it and allow it to hurt you, it will affect your life and the lives of others.

Let's say all that in this sentence. The issues of life flow out of your heart, so keep your heart, attend unto God's words, look diligently at those things that would affect your heart because offenses want to spring up and defile you and others around you.

Do you remember the song, "Another Somebody Done Somebody Wrong Song"? Everybody does somebody wrong. That is just a part of life. You can be different from everybody else because of what you do with what they did to you.

Do not take an offense! Do not ever take an offense—it will tie you up. It will tie up your family. It can even tie up your church.

When he says, "looking diligently ... ," he means to watch for and be able to spot an offense. Sometimes they are very subtle, but sometimes they are not so subtle.

Some people say, "Now, bless your heart, don't be offended by what I'm going to say." That means it is possibly intended to offend! Do not take that offense. You have the chance to decide if you want to take the offense or not. Please do not take it.

Look Out for Others

Hebrews 12:15 in the Wuest translation, William's translation, The Amplified Version, and The Living Bible suggests that we are to look out for other people as well as ourselves.

The Wuest translation says, "...exercising oversight [over yourself] lest anyone be falling away from the grace of God, lest any root of bitterness springing up be troubling you, and through this the many be defiled..."

The William's New Testament says, "Continue to look after one another, that no one fail to gain God's spiritual blessing; or some evil like a bitter root may spring up and trouble you, and many of you be contaminated by it..."

The Living Bible says, "Look after each other so that not one of you will fail to find God's best blessings. Watch out that no bitterness takes root among you, for as it springs up it causes deep trouble, hurting many in their spiritual lives."

The Amplified Version says (I like this one the most), "Exercise foresight and be on the watch to look (after one another), to see that no one falls back from and fails to secure God's grace (His unmerited favor and spiritual blessing), in order that no root of resentment (rancor, bitterness, or hatred) shoots forth and causes trouble and bitter torment, and the many become contaminated and defiled by it..."

These scriptures seem to say that we are to be on guard for any type of offense that is trying to come to our household, or our own personal lives.

We need to guard our heart. I found it interesting that in these translations they talk about guarding our own hearts as well as helping others guard their hearts too. I believe we have a responsibility to caution others if we see the possibility of an offense causing a root of bitterness to grow in them. We always need to say these things in love.

Is there someone close enough to you, husband, wife, or a friend, from whom you could receive something like that? You need to have someone you respect who will tell you the truth. You may not be willing or able to see the root of bitterness forming in your life.

Exercise Foresight

In another translation, "looking diligently" reads, "exercise foresight over these things."

When you exercise foresight, you are paying very close attention to the things going on around you. How you exercise foresight will determine whether a root of bitterness will spring up within you or not. How do you know if there is a root of bitterness springing up in your life?

When you get around someone who has offended you, pay attention to your feelings on the inside. How does that person make you feel?

When you see someone who has offended you coming down the street, do you go to the other side of the street? Or, if they drive by, do you turn away with the excuse of looking to see what fell behind the seat to avoid making eye contact with them?

These are good indicators as to whether or not a root of bitterness is beginning to take form in you. If these things are on the inside of you and if you do not deal with them, they will begin to control you.

I'm not saying this as someone who has not had to deal with it. I have had experience with it. Most of you have had the same kind of experience, so we are talking about getting down to where we live. What do we do with it when it happens?

When we let Jesus become our substitute, all those offenses and those offending people will not affect us because we have cast that care over on Him, and He's taken it so you do not have to. We must let it go. Give it to Jesus.

Dealing with the Roots

People who have come through a tough divorce situation can bring all of that into another relationship. If they do not deal with it, it can follow them into a new relationship.

One particular pastor I knew had a genuine pastor's heart. He was a fine person. He and his wife had some difficulty and they split up. We all know there are two sides to every story. They ended up getting a divorce. He was pastoring a very large church.

After his divorce, the Church Board came to talk to him and told him they wanted to let him go. Because of their fears the board began to control the church. They said, "We are not going to let that happen to us again." When the second pastor started, the board would not give him the freedom to do anything. They pushed him out within a year and a half.

The man who was going to be the third pastor had watched all of this because he was raised in this church. Before they drove out the second man, they had just built a building that cost over a million dollars. Attendance had gone from fifteen hundred to about three thousand in less than six months time, and they were having several services on Sunday morning.

The first thing the new pastor did was to ask the Lord what to teach on. "You know the situation." God told him, "Teach on church government."

So he began to do that. The people got behind him. They loved it but the board did not! The board called a meeting with him after church one Sunday and told him they did not like what he had been teaching. They told him he was taking away from their authority.

He said, "Guys, the people are behind me. You are holding me accountable for the sins of someone else and the situations he created. That's not right. You will drive this church right into the ground by doing that. Either resign today, or I will go three blocks away, start a church, and these people are going to follow me." They did not want to pay for the one and a half million-dollar building, so they all resigned.

I am not teaching on church government; I am simply telling you they carried those offenses through two pastors, and the third pastor had to dig up the root of those offenses or the church would have failed. Those people harbored those offenses and were keeping the church from being progressive.

Offenses carried on like that or carried down through the generations will destroy. So if someone has done you wrong, forget it; drop it! Go on about your life.

Afflictions and Persecutions

Let's look at how offenses affect not only those around us, but what it will do to us personally and how it gets done.

> The sower soweth the word. And these are they by the way side, where the word is sown; but when they have

heard, Satan cometh immediately, and taketh away the word that was sown in their hearts. And these are they likewise which are sown on stony ground; who, when they have heard the word, immediately receive it with gladness; And have no root in themselves, and so endure but for a time: afterward, when affliction or persecution ariseth for the word's sake, immediately they are offended.

Mark 4:14–17 (KJV)

An offense will steal your gladness. All the devil needs to do is to steal your gladness or joy, which is your strength. If he steals your gladness, he won't have to worry about you because your strength will be gone.

Let me say this in regard to offenses. Offenses produce nothing. Offenses produce nothing—they steal.

"Afflictions" and "persecutions" are two areas that Satan uses to cause us to be offended. Through afflictions, personal difficulties, hardships, and life situations there are times that we become offended. Through persecutions or people problems we may become offended.

Why are people persecuting you? The enemy sends them along to harass you. I am convinced there are a lot of Christians who do not know it but they have a timecard in the enemy's file. Satan is thinking "Who shall I try to get offended today? This one is pretty tough so I'll need to send someone they are close to in order to accomplish the task of offending them." People don't necessarily realize they are being used by the enemy, but he knows how to pull their strings to cause them to do his work for him. The person he is using may not understand that they are helping him, but I think in some cases they do.

We take those offenses, and they are designed to steal our gladness. The Word makes you glad. The Word is designed to always produce gladness. When you become glad over the Word, the enemy wants to take it from you. One way he takes it from you is by sending someone across your path to offend you.

If that person, born again or not, Spirit-filled or not, knowing the Word or not, can offend you, he has stolen your gladness. You have decided, "I am going to take this offense. I am offended, he should not have done that to me."

There are things that happen to you every single day that should not happen. If Satan can break through, and grab hold of your soulish man, which is your mind, will, and emotions, and cause you to take that offense, then gladness leaves and his work is done.

With no gladness, faith can be destroyed. Whatever level you are at, whatever degree of faith or degree of spiritual maturity you have gained, gladness is designed to help you. Gladness only comes from the Word, and it is hope to you and your situation.

When you are in a situation that is tough and you get into the Word, the Word begins to give you hope and gladness. That gladness is designed to see you through the situation and bring you out on top.

If you are going through the situation victoriously and are having a great time, the devil wants to step in and steal your gladness by causing an offense to come your way to stop the gladness. If that happens, the enemy has you distressed again. That is exactly what the enemy wants.

The Enemy's Tricks

You know, we give the enemy too much credit. He is really not very smart. It is sad, though, that he seems smarter than a lot of Christians. He only has about five tricks he knows how to play, but we fall for them day in and day out. We think: "How did that happen?" It is the same old thing. He just changed the title and did the same thing again.

In 1974 there was a "discipleship movement" going on. We know there is a term in the Bible called discipleship. It is in there, but some people have gotten a different revelation and take it to the extreme and it destroys people. Many people got out of church because of this discipleship movement. It died off for a period of time, but it came back around in another name. It was the very same thing, just a different name.

All I am saying is—the devil gets as many people as he possibly can with one title, lets it die down for awhile, and goes after something else. A few years later, he comes back with a different title and does the very same thing again to another generation.

It happens all the time. When it happens, we as the body of Christ need to know what the Word says. Who is God? What is the character of God? We need to know if this is an offense that is trying to take place in my life. We need to be sharp enough to see it for what it is.

If we know it goes against the nature of the Word, or the character of God, then we know it is designed to steal our gladness. If anything steals our gladness we can mark it down that it is not God.

Relationships

Have you ever had a really good friendship or relationship destroyed by an offense? Most people have family members this has happened to. If your brothers and sisters, aunts and uncles all enjoy getting together, you are blessed beyond measure!

Relationships are very important. The body of Christ is *relational*. I believe with all of my heart, as we continue to grow in the knowledge of the Word, we will find this true.

Doing things, or having a big vision is important, but in the midst of that you do not want to break off or lose relationships with people. It is pretty hard to accomplish anything with a big vision and no people.

Relationships between husband and wife and family need to be number one priority. It does not matter whether you have a nice house or not. It matters whether you have good relationships with people.

> Then shall thy light break forth as the morning, and thine health shall spring forth speedily: and thy righteousness shall go before thee; the glory of the Lord shall be thy rereward. Then shalt thou call, and the Lord shall answer; thou shalt cry, and he shall say, Here I am. If thou take away from the midst of thee the yoke, the putting forth of the finger, and speaking vanity; And if thou draw out thy soul to the hungry, and satisfy the afflicted soul; then shall thy light rise in obscurity, and thy darkness be as the noon day: And the

Lord shall guide thee continually, and satisfy thy soul in drought, and make fat thy bones: and thou shalt be like a watered garden, and like a spring of water, whose waters fail not." [not lie: those waters don't lie to you] "And they that shall be of thee shall build the old waste places: thou shalt raise up the foundations of many generations; and thou shalt be called, The repairer of the breach, The restorer of paths to dwell in.

Isaiah 58:8–12 (KJV)

This speaks of relationships. Be the repairer of the breach. A breach happens when an offense comes into a relationship. The repairer of the breach is the person who brings that relationship back together again.

You as part of the body of Christ cannot afford to have breaches in your relationships. When there is a breach in a relationship, there is not agreement and you cannot go forward. "The putting forth of the finger," simply means blaming others.

Your Health

Can an offense affect your health? Your health includes your emotional and your physical realms. If you are hurt emotionally and you do not deal with it, it is like a weak spot in an inner tube. As you are pumping air into it, the weakest spot will eventually give and the tube is going to burst.

Let me tell you of a man I once met. I was traveling and had been told to stop in at this man's church while I was passing through. I found his church and attended that night. When I met him, he would not look at me. I did not understand why he would not look at me. This is a man who is respected in the ministry, a man that is called of God.

I found out later that there was a time in his life when he had no idea who his father was and had decided to find him. In his search he also found he had brothers and sisters. They rejoiced in the fact that they found their brother. They knew he was out there, but did not know where. At the same time, he found his father. His father told him, "I wanted your mother to abort you then, and I still wish she had." With that he turned and walked off.

You are going to hurt in a storm like that! I do not care if you have all your armor on. God, in His grace and His mercy, took him under his wings and cared for him for three years while he put it back together.

He was an excellent preacher. He said, "This thing affected me emotionally so much I went blind." For three or four months he could barely see. He told someone, "I would have to stand behind the pulpit and hold on to it and could not see who I was preaching to."

Through the process of time, he has been completely healed of all those past hurts and wounds which were designed to stop him and destroy him and his family's life, and his ministry. He said, "I am not letting it stop me. God will see me through it," and He did!

You may sit there and think, "I can handle it. I can handle it." Can you really?

He took the offense, and it affected him emotionally to the point that it affected him physically. The end result of what the devil wanted to do was to get him out of the ministry and get him out of the soul-winning business. He could have shut it down, all because of an offense.

A gentleman I know who has talked to him since said, "He is healed and doing better than ever!" He has a priority list that is different than it was five years ago. Now his family means more to him than his church.

It would have been easy to hold onto the "he did me wrong"feeling. He could have sung that song 24 hours a day, but he chose to hang onto God. Had he chosen to hold on to his offense, he probably would not be there in his church helping his congregation.

Debt Collectors

Have you heard of a "debt collector" before? You know, they call people and say, "You owe us money." Those debt collectors don't know or care who you are. They say, "Send your money in so I can get my 30 or 40 percent!" But we are not talking about dollars here.

Have you ever had something happen to you and you felt like saying, "I'm going to collect! I'm going to get back at them!"

> After this manner therefore pray ye: Our Father which art in heaven, Hallowed be thy name. Thy kingdom come. Thy will be done in earth, as it is in heaven. Give us this day our daily bread. And forgive us our debts, as we forgive our debtors.
>
> Matthew 6:9–12 (KJV)

You can take your standard from the Lord Jesus Christ, the

one who was offended time after time, and then turned His back on the offenses to minister to the people.

Look at 1 Peter 5:7 (KJV) for a moment, "Casting all your care upon him; for he careth for you." The amount that the Lord can care for you is based on the amount that you cast over on the Lord. If you cast 20% of your care on Him, He can care for you 20%. If you cast 80% over on Him, He can care for you 80%.

If you are going to collect your own debt, you are going to have a rough road to go down! It will use all of your energy in the wrong places, at the wrong times, doing the wrong things.

Jesus became your substitute for everything! When you think someone did you wrong, remember, they did Him wrong first and He took it on Himself. You do not have to bear it.

Quit trying to collect those debts—God does the collecting. Not only that, but if you continue to try to collect debts from people who have wronged you, you will spend your life doing it. It requires the kingdom of God in your life to right those wrongs. An offense ties up the ability of the kingdom of God to operate in your life.

Now look at what Hebrews 11:6 (KJV) tells us, "But without faith it is impossible to please him: for he that cometh to God must believe that he is, and that he is a rewarder of them that diligently seek him." The amount of your cares you cast over on the Lord, determines the amount He can care for you, or the amount He can reward you.

Do you want Him to be your rewarder? Quit trying to collect your own debt! When you begin to try to collect your own debt by saying, "Bless God, I am going to get even with them, they are not going to do this to me." He cannot be your rewarder.

A lady came to the prayer line one time and said, "I caught my husband with another woman last week. Bless God, he is going to pay for it!"

I am not suggesting that he should have been with another woman, but if she is going to keep that attitude, God will be limited in His ability to help or reward her, based on what she has done with the offense.

Bless Your Persecutors

Paul tells us in Romans 12:14 (KJV), "Bless them which persecute you: bless and curse not." There are a lot of times when we think the word "bless" means pulling out our checkbook and writing a check, and giving someone $20. We understand that part of blessing. However, this word "bless' also means, "to speak a blessing over them."

If you want God to get involved in your life to turn situations around, the Word says to speak blessings over those that persecute you and do not curse them.

One of the toughest things that you can go through is when you are sitting with a friend having lunch and they begin to say positive things about the person who offended you. You are sitting there thinking, "I would like to tell them," and you are biting your tongue so nobody will be able to say that you spoke out evil against that person.

Do you know what the sad part is? A lot of times we go ahead and say something. Whenever you and I choose to curse them with our speech, we have limited the Holy One of Israel from getting involved completely in our life and becoming our rewarder and our vindicator.

Watch Your Focus

Have you ever wanted to be vindicated from a wrong you've been falsely accused of? I have. Have you ever retaliated? We all have, from time to time. When you retaliate, do you know what happens? It gives them more fuel. If you walk away from it, the truth will be known.

Who does it hurt worse when you speak out a curse over someone else? Them or you?

Please understand what Romans 10:17 (KJV) tells us, "faith cometh by hearing, and hearing by the Word of God." We've taught that, taught that, and taught that. We say, "If you speak the Word out of your own mouth, your inward ear hears it!"

The same thing happens if you are speaking out a curse. If you speak out curses with your own mouth, your heart hears it, and the very thing that you speak out to curse other people will come back and visit you.

The way you keep this from happening is by not allowing the sins of others to become your focus. If past sins are your focus, they will become a part of your heart. What is in your heart will become a part of your conversation. Matthew 12:34 (KJV) says, "…out of the abundance of the heart the mouth speaketh."

Unforgiveness

Have you thought about why the sins of the father are visited to the third and fourth generation? This happens because those sins have become a part of our conversation. Exodus

20:5 (KJV) tells us, "… visiting the iniquity of the fathers upon the children unto the third and fourth generation…"

Have you ever thought about why an alcoholic father oftentimes has an alcoholic child or grandchild? How do the sins of the father come back and visit the third and fourth generation? By the curse that comes out of their mouth!

What you talk about is going to become a part of you. We can say, "If we are born again we do not have to take on that curse. We can cut that curse off."

That is a true statement. The righteousness of God in Christ is who you are. However, you can be the righteousness of God in Christ Jesus, and if you still curse your father for what he did, it will turn right back and attack you.

Don't Touch God's Anointed

A former pastor shared with me concerning an offense that came against him and his wife when they pastored a small church before they retired. They had approximately 80 people in their church, and their associate pastor's wife decided she could do a better job than they were doing.

She promoted the dissension that destroyed their church. One Sunday they had 80 people in attendance, and the next week they had two show up. You do not want to ever do that to your church or your pastor. She was in her mid-forties and was in good health, but within a year's time she was dead of cancer.

Are you trying to say not to touch God's anointed? Yes, I am. Now I want to clarify something.

Who is God's anointed? The Body of Christ is. You are.

I am. Do you know what that means? It means that you and
I are not to speak against anyone!

UNFORGIVENESS VERSUS FORGIVENESS

We are teaching on unforgiveness versus forgiveness in this chapter. You would be surprised at the things that people get offended over.

I shook a man's hand one time with my left hand because my right one was full. He quit coming to church because I gave him the left hand of fellowship.

"Pastor doesn't like me. He gave me the left hand of fellowship!" Thank God I had my left hand to give! I am just amazed at some of these things.

The Kingdom of God in You

Your kingdom of heaven status has eternal value to you. Your kingdom of God status is you being successful, living a victorious Christian life here on this earth. There are a lot of people who have become born again and have entered into the kingdom of heaven, but they have not learned they can have that victorious life here, which is the kingdom of God within you. (Luke 17:21 KJV)

In Matthew 6:10 (KJV) Jesus was talking about the Lord's prayer, "Thy kingdom come. Thy will be done in earth, as it is in heaven."

In other words, God wants heaven to take place here on earth. However, it is up to you and me whether that happens or not. It is not up to God whether heaven takes place in the earth or not. God set it up that way, and you and I can either help it or hinder it by how we handle offenses.

When offenses are harbored on the inside of us, they stop the flow of the kingdom of God from operating in our lives. Is there anyone of us who can afford, spiritually, physically, socially, emotionally or financially to embrace an offense?

Forgiving and Forgetting

People have said this, "Well, I'm going to forgive you, but I'm not going to forget it!" They have not forgiven either.

You might say, "Well, okay Pastor, if that's the case, then what do I do about all those thoughts of what they did to me?" It is possible for you to cast those thoughts down. Those are imaginations. Imaginations are designed to keep you under pressure and bondage, to keep you in the normal rules and patterns of this world.

But you are not designed to be normal. You are designed to allow the kingdom of God Almighty, Creator of heaven and earth, to live inside of you. When things need to be done, you have the authority and power to get it done because of who you are in Christ.

You and I, through the knowledge of the Word, can take the normal rules and patterns and make them submit to the power of God inside us.

In the area of forgiving and forgetting, there is a place in God that you cannot only forgive but you can also forget. Wouldn't you like to be there?

God Forgives and Forgets

Isaiah 43:25 (KJV) is very enlightening to us, "I, even I, am he that blotteth out thy transgressions for mine own sake, and will not remember thy sins." Notice that God, "will not remember thy sins." Whenever God forgives, He also forgets.

Sin was judged through the death, burial, resurrection, and victorious life of Jesus. When you go to the Father and repent of something, He forgives it. Not only does He forgive it, He forgets it! Why do you suppose He forgets it? Look at those words: "for mine own sake."

"For mine own sake, and will not remember thy sins." Why would God, the creator of the universe say, "I'm going to forgive and forget for my sake"? He knows there is a law that He has put in the universe that says if you do not forgive sin, you retain it.

Think with me for just a moment. Wouldn't it be horrible to serve a God who is retaining all these sins? You would have the wrath of God every day in your life. I thank God for His wisdom. He is smarter than I am, and I sure am glad.

Have you gone to the Lord and said, "Father, forgive me" for something and believed He did? We seem to have problems in our soul believing that God actually forgave us, yet He said He did.

So we run back to the altar and say: "Oh God, forgive me." Then God says, "I do not know what you are talking about. I forgot that." We have this mentality that thinks God never forgets anything. God has chosen to forgive and forget your sins.

Retain or Remit?

John 20:23 (KJV) states that "Whose soever sins ye remit, they are remitted unto them; and whose soever sins ye retain, they are retained." The word "remit" means you have forgiven them. The word "retain" means you have not forgiven them. We could say it this way, "Whose soever sins you retain you attach to you." If this was sin you have chosen not to forgive, then it belongs to you. You are going to hold onto that. It is yours.

Some people say this: "I don't want to be like my mother." "I'll never be like my daddy." The next thing they know, they are exactly like them. They say, "Dear God, the one thing in the world I didn't want was this!" That ought to be an indication to us that they have failed to forgive them.

To me this makes so much sense. It is a spiritual law. If you retain, fail to forgive, fail to loose or let go of the sins of someone else, be it friend, husband, wife, children, parent, or work associates, you are holding on to those things and they become a part of you. You have retained them.

I know this is ministering to someone concerning their parents, or someone who has retained the sins of their father, and it has been eating their lunch. Turn loose of it. Deuteronomy 5:9 (KJV) says that, "I the Lord thy God am a jealous God, visiting the iniquity of the fathers upon the children unto the third and fourth generation of them that hate me."

Any type of unforgiveness is a form of hate, and it will create big problems. In every situation where the Word talks about faith and operating in the principles of faith, the supporting scripture behind it is forgiveness. He is simply saying, "Without forgiveness it won't work."

What Does the Word Produce in You?

Let us look at Mark 11:25 (KJV), "And when ye stand praying, forgive…" Calling those things that be not as though they were [or speaking with your mouth], is the message of faith (Romans 4:17, KJV). Did you know faith and forgiveness are one voice? They are not two voices: they are one.

In order for you to operate successfully in faith, the voice that operates and calls those things which be not as though they were, must also be the same voice that says, "I release and forgive you."

Mark 4:15–20 (KJV) is talking about the sower sowing the Word. We find in verse 20, "And these are they which are sown on good ground; such as hear the word, and receive it, and bring forth fruit, some thirtyfold, some sixty, and some an hundred." The Word can produce 30–60-and 100-fold in our life.

We realize there are some 30–60–100-fold returns financially, but what He wants in your life is 30–60–100-fold Word production. When Jesus is saying the Word produces, He is talking about, "when you stand praying, forgive." That is Word producing in your life.

When you say, "I'm not going to forgive," you are really saying, "I am limiting what the Word can produce in my life because of what they have done to me." That person and what he does or does not do ends up controlling your life!

"Well, not me! God is controlling my life!" If you retain unforgiveness, He is not.

Matthew 18:18–35 (KJV) tells how unforgiveness put two men in prison because of a choice. People are bound because of unforgiveness. When you fail to forgive someone, you are binding yourself and them to some degree.

I know people say, "Well, there isn't anyone who can bind me." Unknown to them, familiar or controlling spirits are working to shatter their lives and keep them in bondage. Through unforgiveness, they open themselves up to the power of these spirits. Unforgiveness has a power that controls the lives of people. Hosea 4:6 (KJV) says, "My people are destroyed for lack of knowledge."

The Seed of Repentance

Matthew 3:8 (KJV) instructs us to "Bring forth therefore fruits meet for repentance:" When the Church sins, and they go to the Father and confess those sins, God the Father is faithful and just to forgive them of those sins, and to cleanse them from all unrighteousness.

1 John 1:9 says if you have sinned and will confess it, He is faithful and just to forgive those sins.

There is a fruit of repentance! Every fruit grows only because there was a seed planted. Charles Capps said, *"We conceive the Word and then we give birth to it."* In human beings there are nine months from the time of conception till the birth takes place. With the seed of the Word of God, there is a conception, a process (or development), and a birth.

We can use that term in a spiritual sense. You have to conceive the Word, allow that Word to become a part of you, nurture it, take care of it, and then, over a period of time, the Word will give birth in your life. It is not up to God how long that time is. It is up to you.

Let us look at repentance. Matthew 3:8 says there is a fruit of repentance. In order to have fruit of repentance, there has to have been a seed of repentance sown. This seed you sow is I John 1:9. "Father, I have sinned. I ask you to forgive me." That is the seed. There have been people who have confessed that seed, but their life-style did not produce it. We have all done that. We have mouthed something, and the seed fell on hard ground. It did not get into the soil.

The Fruit of Repentance

When that seed comes from your heart, and you truly want the fruit of it, there will be a life-style to back that seed up.

"Father, forgive me. I have sinned. I repent." If it is true repentance, the seed of that repentance is going into the soil of your heart, forcing change to come about. Over a period of time you will see the fruit of forgiveness in your life.

I was reading an article about a famous person who made the headlines. The problem was that the man was very jealous. Certain things would happen, and he would either beat his wife, or verbally abuse her, and she would make him leave. He would come back crying and say, "Will you forgive me? I was wrong." She would take him back and he would do it again. This happened over and over.

That was just simply mouthing, "I'm sorry," with no repentance to it whatsoever. There was no substance to it. If there was substance, there would be change, and that change would produce fruit. You would see it.

If you go into business with someone, and they deceive you, they may say, "I'm sorry. Let's go back into business again." But if you go back into business again with them, you either have a lot of money or you are not thinking straight. Maybe this has happened to you. Let me suggest something. Wait to see the fruit of their words before you go back into business with them. It is not really a matter of being super-spiritual, it is just using common sense.

Have you ever watched the movie *Schindler's List?* Schindler was a wealthy German who used all of his money to help free some Jews during the Holocaust in World War II. There were about 1,100 Jews who would have been killed if it had not been for him. He had spent all of his money to free them by the time the war was over. At the end of the movie he still had a big car. He looked at it and he looked at those who were free, and he said, with tears running down his face, "If I would have sold my car it would have been worth 10 more people." He had a pin on his jacket that was apparently solid gold. He took it off and said, "If I would have sold this, it would have been worth two more people."

Consider this. If you have unforgiveness in your heart, you will not think the way he did. You will become selfish. He had repented of even being a German and that repentance bore fruit in the lives of 1,100 Jews.

Repentance Brings Freedom

What we need to do is to come to a place in our lives where we can truly repent and have the fruit of repentance operating in our lives. Then there will be nothing blocking us from what God wants in our lives.

If you have kept unforgiveness in your heart, but now want to let it go, take a moment right now to take care of it.

The first thing is to have a right heart about it then go to the Lord and say, "Father, to the best of my ability, I'm turning this over to you. I've harbored this unforgiveness, this bitterness for years, and it has taken a toll. I don't like it. I don't want it."

Be honest with Him. You cannot lie to God anyway. By an act of faith offer up that person you have held unforgiveness toward by saying, "Father, I forgive them, and I release them now in Jesus' name." If you will do that, you will feel pressure lifted off you, and you will be able to walk in freedom.

We think it does not matter, but it does matter. It matters to your life. There is a freedom that comes with receiving forgiveness that is wonderful.

Do you enjoy being who you really are and just being yourself? There is nothing like it in the world. But if you harbor unforgiveness, you cannot be who you really are, and you are not free.

Having the Peace of God

Look at Colossians 3:15 (KJV), "And let the peace of God rule in your hearts ..." Anytime there is unforgiveness in a person's heart, there is no peace.

There is a difference between peace "with" God and the peace "of" God. Peace "with" God comes when you accept Jesus as your personal Savior. Then the peace "of" God can operate in your life.

But if there is unforgiveness in your heart, the peace of God is not going to be in your life. Unforgiveness destroys the hedge of protection around you, and it can be life threatening.

Judge or Forgive

A man told me he was sent to my church to make sure that everyone did everything right, including me. When this person came to me he said, "The Lord has sent me here be the judge over this whole congregation." I told him, "You are going to have a big job with me!"

I thought to myself, "Then why do we need the Holy Ghost? Holy Ghost, you can go back to heaven, we don't need you here. I have this man to correct the people." Well, that man did not like my answer. He left!

Unforgiveness sets you up as a judge. You and I are not to judge. People say, "Well, I would have never done what that man did." You might have done worse if you were in his shoes. Until you walk in another man's shoes, you do not have anything to say about what he did.

Romans 12:2 (KJV) talks about renewing your mind with the Word and proving "what is that good, and acceptable, and perfect, will of God." The key to destroying unforgiveness is knowledge. You will forgive to the degree that you know you have been forgiven. You will not go beyond that.

Three People You Need to Forgive

There are three people you need to forgive: yourself, others, and God. You may be blaming God for something He did not do. If you do not deal with it, it will begin to destroy you.

Sometimes we find it easier to forgive others than to forgive ourselves. We know we need to forgive others. However, there may come a time in your life when you will need to forgive yourself.

Have you had a bad marriage? Maybe you have had several bad marriages. Maybe you have done something that made you think, "God, how could I have done something so stupid? Father, would you forgive me. I repent right now. I ask you to forgive me."

Did you forgive yourself? If you have not, it will destroy you. The devil will have a heyday in your life. He will keep reminding you of what happened and you will recycle it in your mind day in and day out. Thoughts will come like, "If I would have done this," or "If I would have done that."

You cannot afford to hold unforgiveness toward someone. You cannot afford to hold unforgiveness toward yourself. And, you cannot afford to hold unforgiveness toward God. God is not your problem.

WALKING IN FORGIVENESS

The enemy provides offenses, and then the body of Christ takes those offenses and acts on them. When a Christian takes those offenses and continues to hold on to them, they turn into a root of bitterness. The root of bitterness turns into unforgiveness and then to hate.

Forgiveness is Excusing Others' Faults

After taking the offense, unforgiveness becomes the problem. Unforgiveness has its beginning in an offense.

A borrowed offense is an unnecessary thing. When you borrow an offense from someone, you are obstructing the flow of the kingdom of God in your life. We treat these things like they do not matter, but they do matter. Offenses matter in our lives.

Say this, "Offenses do matter. They have very serious effects on my spiritual life." They ultimately turn into unforgiveness. The word "forgiveness" means "to excuse a fault." Forgiveness is not something anyone deserves. You choose to forgive someone, because of the nature of God in you.

Who forgave first? God did through Jesus Christ. The seed of forgiveness started with God the Father and now is extended to all. He gave His only Son to the world so that no one would have to perish. Jesus Christ was a seed given so people could embrace Him, hold onto Him, and receive Him as their personal Savior.

God stepped beyond what is normal or what is naturally right. He stepped beyond that and in essence said, "You do not deserve this, but I am going to forgive you anyway." The reason He did that is because it is God's nature to forgive. That is the seed God planted into our hearts.

We take the seed we received from God the Father, through Jesus, and then we have a responsibility to do something with it. That seed of forgiveness becomes our nature. The nature of God the Father is inside our recreated spirit because we have accepted Jesus as our personal Savior.

The Nature of God in Us

The nature of God and His forgiveness reside on the inside of your recreated spirit, so you have the ability to forgive. You may not want to. You may say, "I'm not going to do it," but that is beside the point. You do have the ability to forgive if you are born again.

If you are not born again, you do not necessarily have the strength of the inward man to conquer areas of unforgiveness.

Repentance has a seed to it. The seed of repentance is this: "I am sorry." The seed of repentance also has fruit that comes with it. The fruit of repentance is a lifestyle of forgiveness, grace and peace.

Anyone can say, "I am sorry." Saying, "I am sorry," is the beginning. That is planting a seed. We need to plant that seed, keep it in our heart, and allow it to be nurtured and germinate on the inside of us until the fruit of repentance begins to manifest in our lives.

People watch you when you say you are sorry to see whether you are sorry or not. Have you ever forgiven someone and said, "I forgive him or her," but every time you see them, you turn away.

Has your husband or wife ever created a problem for you? You might say, "I forgive you, but I'm not going to talk to you for at least a week." No, you haven't forgiven them.

Don't Collect the Debt!

The word forgiveness means not collecting a debt. We are talking about spiritual debt collecting. Spiritual debt collecting is, "You owe me. I know you did it. I am not going to forget it, and I am going to make you pay."

The problem with that is you cannot pay it. I cannot pay it. No one can pay it back. It is to your advantage and mine to forget it.

Mark 11:25 in the Amplified Bible says, "And whenever you stand praying, if you have anything against anyone, forgive him and let it drop (leave it, let it go), in order that your

Father Who is in heaven may also forgive you your (own) failings and shortcomings and let them drop."

Do you know what we want to do? First, we want to drop the offense, but then we say, "No, wait a minute. I'm going to hold on to that." Then we say, "Well, I'll hurt them. I'm not going to speak to them." No, you have not hurt them. You may hurt their feelings, but you are not hurting them, you are hurting yourself!

Unforgiveness is one of the most damnable things in the body of Christ. It breaks relationships, but more than that, it stops the flow of God from operating in our own personal life.

The Remission of All Punishment Due

W.E. Vine's *Expository Dictionary* says that forgiveness is, "the remission of all punishment due."

Sometimes we say "I forgive you, but I'm going to punish you just a little while." Do you know why we want to punish someone? We are hurting, and if we are hurting, "Bless God," we are going to hurt someone else. Hurting people will hurt other people.

The reason we do that is because we take on those things that have affected us. Maybe someone has come against us, maybe someone's not doing what we think they ought to do, or maybe they said something about us. Whatever the case, we take those things and they become personal to us, when all along, Jesus paid the price for even that! He became the substitute for all of the wrong things and all the bad things people have done to us and said about us. He became the substitute so that you don't have to take them on yourself.

Jesus took those offenses for us. He knew, "If I don't take that offense for them, they'll take it and the things of God won't work in their behalf." We do not want to retain another man's sin because when we do, it becomes ours.

Why Forgive?

Forgive is made of two words: "for" which means "purpose of an activity", and "give" which means "to make a present or offering".

When we forgive someone, it is an activity we engage in and we make an offering toward that person. What we are designed to do is to purposely give an offering of forgiveness to that person for that offense.

> For verily I say unto you, That whosoever shall say unto this mountain, Be thou removed, and be thou cast into the sea; and shall not doubt in his heart, but shall believe that those things which he saith shall come to pass; he shall have whatsoever he saith. Therefore I say unto you, What things soever ye desire, when ye pray, believe that ye receive them, and ye shall have them. And when ye stand praying, forgive, if ye have ought against any: that your Father also which is in heaven may forgive you your trespasses. But if ye do not forgive, neither will your Father which is in heaven forgive your trespasses.
>
> Mark 11:23–26 (KJV)

The first reason to forgive is that God said to. He did not suggest that you forgive. He did not say, "Well, I think it's in your best interest if you do forgive," or, "I understand the situation and if you can find it in your heart to forgive, maybe you should." He doesn't say that. He said, "When you stand praying, forgive, if you have ought against any:" (Mark 11:25, KJV).

The Shield of Faith

The second reason to forgive is so our faith will work. It is your faith that brings the supernatural into the natural. If you have held onto unforgiveness, the supernatural quits flowing through you. Unforgiveness affects your faith.

Ephesians 6:12–17 talks about the full armor of God. Part of the armor is the shield of faith. Another part of the armor is the sword of the Spirit, which is the spoken word. The sword is an offensive weapon. The shield is a defensive weapon. Your shield of faith is designed as a protective mechanism. It is a defensive weapon that protects you.

There is a part of your body that doesn't work with unforgiveness. It is your arm that holds up the shield of faith. You can be on the offensive with the sword of the Spirit, confess the Word, and speak very boldly. Everyone will think, "Hallelujah, that man knows the Word," but if you are not protecting yourself with the shield of faith, the weapons of the enemy will affect you and will stick into your body. They will drain the life of God out of you.

When you are not operating in forgiveness, your arm is not holding up the shield of faith. The life of God will drain out because of all the offenses that you receive into your life.

Your faith is a protective shield. Without it you can and will receive the offenses the enemy brings to your life. Often you face the enemy with your sword drawn, speaking the

Word out over the situation, and yet the attacks of the enemy continue to come at you. If you have unforgiveness in your heart, your shield is not working effectively. The fiery darts of the enemy will penetrate into your soulish realm and will affect the way you look at things.

I am simply saying, you cannot afford to do that. You cannot afford to sit there and harbor unforgiveness in your own heart. I don't care if you own all the money in your town; you cannot afford to do it. Offenses and unforgiveness can kill you. The ultimate goal of the enemy is to bury you with offenses so you will quit breathing.

Notice what Mark 11:26 (KJV) says. "But if you do not forgive, neither will your Father which is in heaven forgive your trespasses." I don't know about you, but that seems pretty stout to me. So, can you afford to hold onto forgiveness? I don't think you can. Unforgiveness is something that will eat your lunch, and you'll not even know what happened.

Cleansed from all Spiritual Filthiness

The third reason to forgive is that unforgiveness is spiritual filth. Ephesians 5:26 (KJV) states, "That he might sanctify and cleanse it with the washing of water by the word." Unforgiveness is spiritual filthiness. The way that you get cleansed is through the Word of God. The Spirit of the Word constantly washes you, cleansing you from spiritual filth.

People ask, "Why do you always suggest that people enter into the presence of God?" Whenever you are in the presence of God all of that unforgiveness begins to melt away on the inside of you. Sometimes people avoid entering into the presence of God because they want to retain these things. If they will go into His presence those things will begin to melt away. What will they have to talk about then? They say, "This thing has controlled my life. What would I do if I was free?" You would be blessed beyond measure.

You say, "But I haven't collected my full debt yet." I have news for you! You are not going to. It will probably collect you!

Free from Torment

Reason number four to forgive is to avoid torment in your own life. Matthew 18:33–35 tells about the servant who owed his lord some money, and the lord forgave him. Then the servant found someone that owed him some money, and he grabbed him by the neck and threw him in jail.

> Shouldest not thou also have had compassion on thy fellowservant, even as I had pity on thee? And his lord was wroth, and delivered him to the tormentors, till he should pay all that was due unto him. So likewise shall my heavenly Father do also unto you, if ye from your hearts forgive not every one his brother their trespasses.
>
> Matthew 18:33–35 (KJV)

Do you know what the tormentors are? When you and I fail to forgive we are setting a spiritual law into motion.

God is not tormenting you. The law of unforgiveness is tormenting you. The law of unforgiveness will literally cause you to be subject to the tormentors and to the situations or circumstances of life. I do not know about you, but I have enough problems in my own personal life dealing with different situations. I do not need something else to deal with.

We talk about faith and how faith builds in our hearts. We speak the Word and hear ourselves say it, and our faith or confidence becomes stronger. But flip the coin over. The other side of that coin is that unforgiveness harbored in your heart causes you to speak the wrong things. Hearing ourselves say the wrong things feeds the unforgiveness, and it becomes stronger. The law of unforgiveness takes you by the arm and leads you to prison.

One real problem with family situations is that if you ever get unforgiveness started, it will tear your whole family apart. You know what I'm talking about. You don't want that. You are not responsible for the other person's actions. If there is anything at all that you can do, instead of trying to avoid it, try to smooth it out.

Some of you have had friends and family, even your best friends, turn on you. Forget it! Drop it! Why did they do it? I don't know. They probably did it because they were hurting, or sometimes it's because of greed. A lot of family situations are created over an inheritance. Greed enters in and causes offenses, bitterness, and unforgiveness. It stops the whole relationship.

Forfeiting Ground

We, as the body of Christ, have a responsibility to the Lord to take ground from the enemy. We are designed and given a commission to take that ground!

We are to take his ground. Do you know what happens? We begin to take ground, and we are really doing well. All of a sudden offenses, unforgiveness, and a root of bitterness come in. Instead of taking ground, we forfeit the ground. We give it back to the devil. Unforgiveness steals more ground from the body of Christ than probably anything on this earth.

We say, "Let's take the community." If we are walking in unforgiveness, we are not going to take it. I am not just talking about a church group or a family group. If two are walking in unforgiveness with each other they are limited in what they can do. If you and your spouse are walking around in unforgiveness, you are literally limited in what God can do through your life. You are not taking ground; you are giving it up.

Obtaining Revelation Knowledge

The fifth reason to forgive is so your personal relationship with God is not blocked. Matthew 5:8 (KJV) says, "Blessed are the pure in heart; for they shall see God." The pure in heart simply means those who deal with sin. Blessed are they that deal with sin. In other words, they stay on top of sin. They don't let it get a hold in their life.

"For they shall see God." The word, "see" means "to perceive." Another translation reads like this, "For they shall obtain revelation knowledge."

If you and I fail to deal with sin, we fail to obtain revelation knowledge of the Word of God. When you and I fail to obtain revelation knowledge of the Word of God, we are cutting off the flow from heaven itself down to our lives. We cannot afford to do that.

Walking in Love

Reason number six to forgive is so you can walk in love. Ephesians 5:2 (KJV) tells us "... walk in love, as Christ also hath loved us ..." You cannot truly walk in love without forgiving.

People who have been divorced must be careful to make sure they forgive their ex-spouse. If you fail to forgive and go into another marriage you will bring all of your unsettled issues into your new marriage, and they will eventually surface. Whatever you brought into your marriage, is what's in it.

If you are a woman reading this and you have not had a good relationship with your father, you must be careful. You may be expecting your husband to be able to fill the void left from your childhood. Whatever the relationship between a parent and a child, if the grownup child is not careful, he or she will bring that type of relationship problem into a marriage. If the relationship is not under the grace of God, or under the authority of the Word, the marriage will be affected.

If you brought all the garbage from the past into your marriage, you need to deal with it. Through unforgiveness you are retaining the sins of another person, pulling them into your life, and mixing those very sins into your present situation. By releasing the things you are holding against other people, you cause these things to leave your life.

Whatever is in your heart will be revealed. People say, "Well, I've had this situation for years and years and it hasn't affected me." But it has, and is, and will continue to affect your life until your heart is changed! Until the heart is changed, you will keep doing things to cover the pain. Release the people in your past, so you can walk in love toward those in your present. There is a place in God where you can say, "it just doesn't hurt anymore."

Have a maintenance check of your own life, of your own heart. Look into your heart. Exercise spiritual foresight. This is an opportunity for me to be offended. I believe I'll refuse."

2 Timothy 2:25 (KJV) says that we "oppose ourselves." The devil comes and beats us over the head. We get so used to it that when he quits, we continue to beat ourselves over the head!

That's what happens with unforgiveness! We blame the devil and say, "It's his fault that I'm walking in unforgiveness." It is not his fault—it is ours. We have to make a quality decision to change what we are doing.

Holding the Advantage

> To whom ye forgive any thing, I forgive also: for if I forgave any thing, to whom I forgave it, for your sakes forgave I it in the person of Christ; Lest Satan should get an advantage of us: for we are not ignorant of his devices.
>
> 2 Corinthians 2:10–11 (KJV)

The Amplified Bible says, "…To keep Satan from getting the advantage over us." *Reason number seven to forgive is so that Satan cannot get an advantage over us.*

People ask, "Well, how important is it?" Do you want to serve the circumstances of life, or do you want to serve God? Do you want God to be your rewarder, or do you want the devil to be your rewarder? Do you want circumstances to rule your life, or do you want to rule the circumstances? Do you want to walk in the love of God, or do you want to walk in bitterness?

Look at Ephesians 4:26–27 (KJV), "Be ye angry, and sin not: let not the sun go down upon your wrath: Neither give place to the devil." Do you know that you can be angry and not sin? There is nothing wrong with being angry at the devil, but when you are angry, make sure your anger is aimed at him and what he has done.

When someone offends you on purpose, or they do something to you on purpose, you know it is a direct attack. Understand that the base of the operation comes from the devil, not from the person. Look beyond the situation and see the true source.

Ephesians 4:27 (KJV) goes on and says, "Neither give place to the devil." In one translation the word "place" reads, "a foothold." A foothold in the Greek means, "a base of operations." When you and I stand in unforgiveness we have given the devil, "a base of operation" to come in and work from that base and affect our whole life.

Receiving the Wisdom of God

The devil's number one way to keep you from doing the things of God is to offer you an offense. If you take it, or become offended, that offense turns to a root of bitterness. The way you can tell if there is a root of bitterness is by simply listening to what you are saying. Another way you can tell that there is a root of bitterness is by how you react toward those who offended you when you see them, or what you say when their name is brought up.

Some time ago, a gentleman and I were talking, and he brought up a name I had not expected to hear. Before I knew what was happening, my blood was boiling! I started to tell him exactly what I thought, and I then remembered, "I don't think I can afford to do that. I think I better deal with it."

If you just sit back, take a few moments of time and ask the Spirit of God to give you the wisdom about something, He will give it to you!

If you go in your own wisdom and strength, the reaction of your blood boiling will not be to your advantage. Do you know that when you get really angry and your blood boils about situations, particularly offensive situations, you say and do the wrong thing? Let God give you the wisdom you need to stay cool.

DEVELOPING CHARACTER

My prayer for this book is that it will minister to your heart, and you will see the significance of offenses and developing character.

Character is something on the inside of us. The real person lives on the inside. We are going to look at that in this chapter. In addition, we will look at the area of the senses.

We have shown how offenses lead to a root of bitterness, and a root of bitterness leads to unforgiveness, and the unforgiveness ultimately leads to hatred.

A Target for the Enemy

We would say a Spirit-filled, Bible-reading Christian could not have any hatred in their heart, but you are the exact target the enemy is aiming for! You have some insight in the Word that is beginning to minister to you and set you free. The enemy wants to steal that from you in any way he can.

His strategy is to offer you an opportunity to be offended, walk in unforgiveness and ultimately hatred. It's up to you whether you take the offense or not.

Some say, "The devil made me do it." No, we blame a lot of things on the devil that are not his fault. He has put a plan into motion, in this world system, to defeat you. God has put a system into motion, in the spirit realm, that will cause you to be successful. It is called forgiveness.

The Word says in Joshua 24:15 (KJV), "choose you this day whom you will serve." If you decide to choose the offense, the devil's not stealing from you—you are stealing from yourself.

If you decide to choose the life of God (to bury and forget those offenses), although it may hurt and put pressure on you in certain situations of your life, you will be glad you said, "I'm not going to take that. I'm going to live for God. I know what they said, but I'm not going to hold on to it."

The Greek word for offense is the word "scandalon" and it means "bait." You remember the story, "Get your hand out of the cage, monkey!" We think, "How foolish that is!"

Delivered from Offenses

We may boast that we believe the Word in it's entirety. However, the blood that delivered us from sin, sickness and disease is the same blood that delivered us from offenses. And yet we hold onto offenses!

Hebrews 12:15 (KJV) talks about looking diligently"...lest any root of bitterness springing up trouble you, and thereby many be defiled." People say, "Well, it's just my problem and it's not going to affect anyone." If you take an offense, it troubles or torments you, and then it produces a root of bitterness. While it is your problem, you will begin to give offenses to many other people. Defiled in this verse means contaminated. Your offense will contaminate and affect other people. You and I are here to build people, not to tear them down.

Sometimes we want to go into someone else's home and try to correct them. Do not go into someone's home and create an offense. That is their sanctuary. You don't need to do that to anyone. But you say, "They need to know!" Pray that God will tell them. There may be an opportunity by the Spirit for you to speak into their life, but if so, the Spirit of God will also give you the way to do it so no one will be offended.

The Spirit of Truth

It is not always what you say that affects people. It is how you say it! Some people say, "Well, we want the truth."

There is a legal side to truth, but what is needed is the spirit-side of truth. The spirit-side of truth will set people free and minister life to them. The legal side is cut and dried and can cause an offense. It is the Spirit of Truth coming out of your mouth that will minister to people.

Until you have taken an offense, you do not have an offense to give. If you have given an offense, it is simply because there is an offense inside you. It could be called a grudge.

We think a grudge is cute when it's a baby. We like to lift it up and show it off. When you were a small child, you could be lifted up and down easily. If you have a grudge and lift it up and set it back down often enough, it is not so cute anymore. Cute gets old after a while. The older it gets, the heavier it gets. It will weigh you down and hinder you. We take these cute little grudges and hold on to them until they tear us apart, physically, spiritually, emotionally, socially and financially.

A borrowed offense is something that does not pertain to you at all; it is none of your business. "Bless God, I'm going to make it mine." If you recall, I took an offense that wasn't mine. Have you taken an offense that was not yours?

Going to the Grocery Store

We go to the grocery store and pick out the best food for our family. We never buy arsenic. We would never do that. Often times our spiritual life is like going to the grocery store. We decide, "Do I want to serve this offense, or do I want to serve this blessing?" What we show our children is what we are serving them. We either show them the grace of God, the life of God, or we show them some poison such as an offense.

When we begin to demonstrate offenses, a root of bitterness enters in and all that comes out of us are those types of things, and this is what our children are being served. We wonder, "Why did my child grow up to be this way?" It is because that is what we have demonstrated to him.

Some people ask, "Well, how did he get that way? I always took him to church. I always went with him to church." Time out! Going to church or sending them to church is fine and great, but what really counts is your instruction in the home. When your children see you take offenses and give offenses, you mark it down, they will pick up those things and they will become offensive to people.

Obtaining the Things of God

The way to obtain the things of God is to refuse the offense when it comes. You need to be healed. You need to have all your bills paid. You need to have a peaceful home. You need all these things rather than any offense.

We use the term, "getting on the bandwagon." If the bandwagon has good things on it, hop on! If it has something that will destroy you, leave the "bandwagon" alone. Let it roll away from you!

We talked about how offenses stop the flow of the kingdom of God in our lives. The kingdom of God refers to your abundant life here on this earth.

"Well, Pastor, I'm born again and Spirit filled. Taking an offense will not keep me out of heaven." However, taking an offense will keep you from operating in the fullness of the kingdom of God here on this earth! The degree to which we take an offense is the degree to which we will stop the flow of the kingdom of God from operating in our lives.

A minister friend of mine said, "A person that is deceived does not know he is deceived because he is deceived."

Have you truly, with a pure heart, tried to get someone to see a problem in their life, in their character, and they just cannot see it? We need to keep our hearts pure before God so He can minister the truth to us, and so we can see it.

You are designed to be free from sickness, disease, poverty, pain, confusion, etc. You are also designed to be free from offenses. Your physical and emotional systems cannot function properly under an offense. They just cannot do it. We need to come to a place that nothing offends us.

An offense is a form of selfishness. I want you to read

that again. An offense is a form of selfishness. It means you are more concerned with yourself than with others. What we ought to do is to look beyond the fault and see the need. Our tendency is to not see the need, only the fault. We are very quick to point out someone else's fault.

Faith Under Pressure

In order to have the patience to get through a situation, you need to see the end result. The only way you are going to find the end result of what you are going through will be to take a stand (Ephesians 6:13). Get into the presence of God and stay there. Seek His face in this particular situation, and He will show you the end result of it. This enables you to stand. Seeing the end result will cause you to have the strength and patience to get through it.

The only reason Jesus was able to endure the cross is because He stayed in the presence of God in the Garden of Gethsemane, and He prayed to the point that His sweat was as drops of blood. He prayed fervently and He saw, in that prayer time, the joy that was set before Him and was able to endure the cross.

When you make a covenant decision with the Lord to literally stay before Him until you see the end result, you will be able to walk through your situation and it will not pull you down.

We ask, "Well, why are there are so many opportunities to be offended?" It is Satan's number one weapon against you. If he can offend you, he can stop the flow of God in your life.

Having the opportunity to be offended is not the problem. The problem is taking the offense. Having a thought go through the mind that is negative or contrary to the Word is not a problem. It is taking that thought or capturing it that becomes the problem.

Mark 4:9 (KJV) says, "He [Jesus] said to them, he that hath ears to hear, let him hear!" The Greek says, "Let him keep on hearing." May I put a little different spin on it? "He that hath ears to hear, let him keep on looking and hearing diligently."

The Real You Shows Up

Now look at James 1:2 (KJV), "My brethren, count it all joy when you fall into divers temptations." The word temptation there simply means tests and trials, difficulties, things you face. Now, generally speaking, we identify tests and trials with circumstances. Do you know why there are circumstances? Because there are people. There are circumstances of life designed by the enemy to keep us from flowing in the things of God.

James 1:2 in The Message Bible says, "Consider it a sheer gift, friends, when tests and challenges come at you from all sides. You know that under pressure, your faith-life is forced into the open and shows its true colors. So don't try to get out of anything prematurely. Let it do its work so you become mature and well-developed, not deficient in any way."

All the pressures of life are attacks against your soulish man (your mind, will, emotions, thoughts, and feelings) to get a response. Your response reveals your character and the maturity level of your faith.

The pressures of certain situations are often the things we want to run from, but when we run from them, we are not developing character.

Shallow Soil of Character

Mark 4:16–17 in The Message Bible reads this way, "And some are like the seed that lands in the gravel. When they first hear the Word, they respond with great enthusiasm. But there is such shallow soil of character that when the emotions wear off and some difficulty arrives, there is nothing to show for it."

As you and I go through this life, we need to have something to show for it. How we handle offenses greatly determines the Word that we are able to show in our lives. This will reveal whether we are living our lives in our own strength, or in the strength of the Lord.

Here in The Message Bible it says there is such shallow soil of character, that when the emotions wear off and some difficulties arrive, there is nothing to show for it. When there is shallow soil of character people are led by their emotions. Being led by your emotions is like building your house on sand. When we face difficult situations, and we have no character, fortitude, self-discipline, or moral excellence, there will be nothing left to show.

The word "character" has to do with "integrity, honesty, what you are when the charisma wears off, and who you are in private." Webster's definition of "character" is "essential quality, an individual's pattern of behavior or personality, moral constitution, moral strength, self-discipline or fortitude."

When You Fall into Temptation

In James 1:2 (KJV) it says, "My brethren, count it all joy when ye fall into divers temptations." It does not say, "*if* you fall ..." It says, "when you fall ..."

There has been some teaching in the past that when you become a Christian there will be no adversity that comes your way. That is contrary to normal thinking. Picture yourself in a boat in the stream of life. When you accept Jesus as your personal Savior, you turn and you start rowing in the other direction. The more radical you become in your stand for the Word, the more you go against the current. You will live life standing and working against adversity.

It is not "if" the tests and trials come, it is "when" they come. No one likes them, but the tests and trials of life develop your character. You find out who you are through them. Your character is supposed to manage your emotions so you will have increase. If we do not manage our emotions, we will have decrease.

Every member of the body of Christ has been designed to be completely free in every situation we encounter. The only limitation we have is our thinking. If we would begin to think like God thinks, we would be free.

The Methods of the Enemy

The sower soweth the word. And these are they by the way side, where the word is sown; but when they have heard, Satan cometh immediately, and taketh away the word that was sown in their hearts. And these are they likewise which are sown on stony ground; who, when they have heard the word, immediately receive it with gladness; [or enthusiasm] And have no root in themselves, and so endure [or allow patience to operate] but for a time: afterward, when affliction or persecution ariseth for the word's sake, immediately they are offended.

Mark 4:14–17 (KJV)

There are five areas the devil uses against us to keep us from operating in the things of God: (1) affliction (2) persecution (3) cares of this world (4) deceitfulness of riches (5) and lust of other things.

The devil does not have any new tricks. He uses the same ones over and over. He changes the recipe a little and says, "Here is something new." It is not new—it is the same thing.

There is no new way of getting free. The only way is submitting to the Lord Jesus Christ and allowing the Word to penetrate your heart. That is how freedom comes. Jesus paid the price for it all. When Jesus paid the price for the brokenhearted, He paid the price for all broken hearts. Your broken heart is not one that He has no answer for. He paid the price for yours, also.

Look Out for Offenses

Look at Mark 4: 16,17 (KJV) again. "These are they likewise which are sown on stony ground; who … when affliction or persecution ariseth for the word's sake, immediately they are offended." Afflictions are circumstances, hardships and difficult situations. Persecutions have to do with people or relational problems.

When afflictions and persecutions arise, immediately they bring an offense. When you get to the bottom of it, afflictions are created because of people. They are people based. Often times we do not see it that way. We just see the circumstances we face. We know persecutions are people related. Through afflictions or persecutions people become offended.

The reason people become offended is because they have no root in themselves. They have no root system because the seed of the Word was not sown in good ground. It was sown in stony ground. Our soulish realm or our heart is the soil. A root system is established in our soil by hearing and hearing and hearing the Word or the seed. The stones in the soil are the offenses, the anger, the unforgiveness we retain.

Inside and Outside

Jesus said in Mark 4:18–19 (KJV), "And these are they which are sown among thorns; such as hear the word, And the cares of this world, and the deceitfulness of riches, and the lusts of other things entering in, choke the word, and it becometh unfruitful."

If you have a thorn bush, there has to be some soil for it to have grown there. Praise God, at least there is some soil.

The cares of this world, the deceitfulness of riches and the lust of other things are three areas that have to do with who you are in your heart, and how you deal with life.

The afflictions and persecutions come from the outside. You have no control over whether these things happen or do not happen to you.

Verse 18 says there are some thorns out there. Our heart is the soil. The reason people have thorns growing in the soil of their heart is because they have taken on the cares of this world, the deceitfulness of riches, and the lusts of other things. Those three areas steal from us inwardly.

Paul Warns the Church

> Take heed therefore unto yourselves, and to all the flock,
> over which the Holy Ghost has made you overseers, to
> feed the church of God, which He hath purchased with
> His own blood. For I know this, that after my departing
> shall grievous wolves enter in among you, not sparing
> the flock. *[Attack comes from the outside.]* Also of your own
> selves shall men arise, speaking perverse things, to draw
> away disciples after them. *[Attack comes from within.]*
>
> Acts 20:28–30 (KJV)

Paul is writing to the Church of Ephesus here. People are the
Church. The church is not a building. The enemy comes at
the Church two ways. The devil attacks from the outside, but
he also attacks from the inside.

The afflictions and persecution are outward, but he also
wants to attack you on the inside. Your character begins on the
inside and produces to the outside. If the soil of your character
is shallow, then Satan can throw situations across your path and
you will take hold of them. The cares of this world, deceitfulness of riches and lust of other things will enter in, and it will
begin to choke out the Word of God on the inside of you.

Beware of Inward Attacks

The church can handle the outward attacks. You do not
destroy the church by making some new legislation. If Satan
wants to destroy the church he goes to the inside.

I was talking to a pastor friend of mine who took a church,
and when he got there it was a mess. It was a large church that had

about 1,200 on the membership roll, but only about 600 attended. Half of those 600 were New Age people. When the New Age movement filtered into the church, it became a mess!

He just preached the Word. He stood against the New Age people and preached the Word. It got down to 300 people in the first nine months. It was a tough time for him, but he kept preaching the Word, and finally, he began to see the light at the end of the tunnel.

He said that the last nine months had been pure blessing. They have grown back up to 500 people, and all of the New Age people are gone. God has a strong core there now.

I know of another pastor who had a church of 7,000 at one time. When a man has a church of 7,000, you assume he is doing something right! The enemy is looking for those who are doing things right. It does not matter what size the church is, 50 or 50,000.

One day a lady came in and wanted to have an intercessory prayer group. She was a New Age person, but nobody checked her out, and in a year's time the church had gone down to 1,500 people. Why did that happen? Because the enemy got on the inside of the four walls of the church.

Character - Who You Are on the Inside

We are talking about you and me personally because we are the church.

We are talking about who you are on the inside. If you are easily offended, your soil is not very deep. The bottom line is, "Who are you? How deep does your soil run?"

People say this, "Pastor, they are coming against me." Hey,

that is just the way a lot of things are. The problem is not that they are coming against you, but how you are handling it.

Facing Rejection

One of the biggest problems you and I will face is rejection. We do not want someone to not like us. We might say, "I don't care if they don't like me," and there may be an element of bravery in that statement.

When someone rejects us or comes against us, it is a personal wound and we feel we have been stabbed in the heart. If we don't learn to deal with rejection we are choosing to be offended.

We can say, "I'm not offended, I'm not offended, I'm not offended," only to find we are offended and there is a bitterness in us that has caused us to refuse to forgive people or to almost hate them.

If you and I fail to develop character on the inside of us, we will so easily take on those offenses, develop them on the inside of us and be defeated in our lives. Why does Satan want that? He wants to stop the flow of the kingdom of God from operating in your life so that your life will be miserable.

We are not designed to be miserable. We are not supposed to be miserable one day of our lives! Jesus paid the price for our misery. He shed His blood so we don't have to be miserable; so we can enjoy life. We must learn to quit being offended.

I would rather receive the blessings of God than to take what the devil wants for me. We think we can take an offense and then ask God to bless us. But He can't.

THE LAW OF CONFESSION

We refer to the law of confession as a positive confession. We speak the Word and we call it a positive confession, but it really is the law of confession.

The Fruit of Your Lips

Your confession activates a spiritual law. When you speak a positive statement out of your mouth, you begin to believe it, and it goes to work on your behalf. It begins to surround you, and brings changes to your life.

The other side of confession is that your negative statements can work against you and bring changes you don't want. If you're offended, your confession will be full of bitterness, and it will put you in bondage. It is a law.

Proverbs 18:21 (KJV) says, "Death and life are in the power of the tongue: and they that love it shall eat the fruit thereof." Notice it says both death and life are in the power of your tongue. Then it says, "They that love it shall eat the fruit thereof." Also Isaiah 57:19 says, "I create the fruit of the lips."

Matthew 6:21 (KJV) says, "For where your treasure is, there will your heart be also". If your heart treasures an offense, you will know it by the words that come out of your mouth.

Don't think what you say doesn't matter because it does. You are affecting yourself. The Bible says, "death and life lie in the power of the tongue..." This is the law of confession.

Speaking the Word of God

Romans 10:17 (KJV) says, "So then faith cometh by hearing, and hearing by the Word of God." I like to say this, "faith cometh by hearing, and hearing, and hearing and hearing..." If faith cometh by hearing, how do you suppose fear comes? By hearing the negative.

When you speak the Word, you retain 90% of what you are hearing yourself say. When someone else speaks the Word to you, you are retaining 10% of what you are hearing them say. If you speak the Word of faith, your inner ears are hearing you speak and it becomes a greater part of you. You are retaining about 90% because you are saying it.

When you confess the Word, it means more to you than if I tell you what the Word says. It is not what someone else says that makes you different. It is what you say that makes you different. So when you speak the Word, you are retaining 90% of what you are hearing yourself say. If that is true, what about the other side of confession?

When you take an offense, that offense ultimately ends up being voiced doesn't it? It turns into a root of bitterness.

An offense turned into a root of bitterness will always be voiced. A root of bitterness produces wrath. Wrath refers to the words coming out of your mouth.

Romans 12:14 (KJV) says, "Bless them which persecute you: bless, and curse not." The word "bless" here means "to bless them with your speech, to speak well of another." The word "curse" means "to speak evil of another."

Your Words Become a Part of You

There is a law of confession, and when you speak the Word or a blessing, that confession becomes a part of who you are. When you curse or speak evil of another, that confession becomes part of you. This is also the law of confession at work. Death and life are in the power of the tongue. So with the authority and power of your tongue, either you have chosen to speak life to yourself and others, or you have chosen to speak cursing to yourself and others.

When you speak good or bad, blessing or cursing, you are retaining 90% of it. Cursing means to speak evil of. If you speak evil or curse another person, do you know what is happening? You are causing that very thing to come to you!

Free to be Who You Were Designed to be

A positive confession brings happiness. Blessing produces happiness. Cursing produces depression. Were you raised in a home where the mother or the father, or both, constantly downgraded everyone in the family, the neighbors, or anyone? Do you know someone who was?

The reason those kinds of things were said was because

someone was hurt. Hurting people always hurt others. If we surround ourselves with these types of words, we end up being a depressed person. We may smile on the outside, but we are crying on the inside.

I was talking to a gentleman who said he had a friend with a wonderful family. He had a good job and made more than enough to support his family. He had four tremendous teen-age boys and everything to look forward to. This man battled with constant put-downs from his mother and father for years. He never did win their acceptance. Finally one day he just put a gun to his head and said, "I'm not going to go any further."

I am talking about you being free to be who you are; or who you were designed to be. You and I were never designed to be depressed. Never!

Have ever you thought, "God just made me that way?" God did not make you that way.

The law of confession works both ways. When you speak blessings, you will be blessed; when you curse, you will retain that cursing.

Do not let what your parents did or said control you now. Don't retain or embrace the words of cursing that were spoken over you, or you will reproduce them in your own life.

If you are, stop right now and take it to God. Forgive them and accept God's love into your heart, and begin to let that forgiveness and love change you today. Let your heart mend, and your speech will follow. If you have a friend who is in this situation, minister life to them instead of borrowing their offense.

Offenses can Lead to Rebellion

Up to this point we have been talking about ignorance of the Word. Now we are going to look at rebellion. These are two things God cannot bless: ignorance and rebellion.

Here are five steps that will take you directly to rebellion: (1) taking an offense (2) leads to complaining (3) leads to forgetting your calling (4) leads to comparing gifts (5) leads to undermining leadership or authority. I am not suggesting you take these steps. Please don't!

Undermining leadership is rebellion. If you are rebellious, God cannot bless you, nor will you bless others. It is not going to happen.

Some of us have heartaches today because of rebellion. We may have let our children rebel and did not correct them, or we may have rebelled against our own parents and carried this rebellion into our present life.

Rebellion disrupts your peace, and we are designed to be men and women of peace. Your system cannot handle rebellion. It is not designed to, should not have to and will not do it.

A Place of Refuge

> Behold, bless ye the Lord, all ye servants of the Lord, which by night stand in the house of the Lord. Lift up your hands in the sanctuary, and bless the Lord. The Lord who made heaven and earth bless thee out of Zion.
>
> Psalms 134:1–3 (KJV)

The word "sanctuary" in *Webster's Dictionary* means "a place of refuge." It also means a shelter or protection from danger.

Every person wants and needs a sanctuary. If your sanctuary or your place of protection is only in church on Sunday mornings, it is not supposed to be that way. It is supposed to be in your home Monday through Saturday also. Your home is meant to be your sanctuary.

What am I getting at when I am talking about needing a place of protection, a sanctuary, or a place of refuge? When you go home at night, you may have had a busy day or a bad day at work. Do you know what you need? You need a place of protection. You may live by yourself, or you may live in a home with children and a spouse, but that home needs to be a place of protection, sanctuary, and refuge.

Do you know there are a lot of people whose homes are not a place of protection or a sanctuary?

Do you remember the theme song to a program that used to be on TV with a bar-type of atmosphere, "a place where everyone knows your name?" Places like that are a refuge for a lot of people. It is their only protection. They are in the place where everyone knows their name.

The bartender is the world's pastor. He knows exactly what Norm needs. When Norm enters the door, what happens? Everyone says, "Norm!" Then they all cheer, "Norm's here! What will it be, Norm? The same?"

Norm did not have a sanctuary at home. He had one at the local bar. They didn't talk bad about him. What I am saying is that your home needs to be a place of protection, a place you want to run to and where you can hide. If it is not, mark it down, you will find a sanctuary somewhere.

Perhaps it will be in another person's arms. If your sanctuary is not your home, you will find someone who offers theirs.

What does that have to do with offenses? Your system cannot handle it if there are offensive actions and words constantly occuring in your home. You do not want to handle it. It will affect every area of your life and wear you out.

Guard Your Sanctuary

One family we knew had children that ran wild in their home. They cartwheeled over the top of the new furniture or did whatever. That is not what we do in our home. That is not how we live. In their sanctuary, if it makes them comfortable, fine, but we don't want that confusion in the atmosphere of our home.

Sometimes people take an offense, and then they want to come and spew out their poisonous trash in your sanctuary. Their words, positive or negative, are going into the spirit realm and affecting the atmosphere in your home. You ask, "Well, that doesn't have any effect on my home, does it?"

Whether you speak faith-filled words or cursings, there is an atmosphere that settles into your sanctuary, and affects the operation of that sanctuary. Does that matter? Sure it does.

When you live under the pressure of an offense, you become depressed and it does affect your life. When you are offended, do not go into another man's sanctuary and use it as a garbage dump. There is a difference in being ministered to and just dumping your garbage in someone's sanctuary.

One day a woman walked into our house and created quite a stir. She had not been there two minutes till my wife said, "This is my sanctuary, and I'll not have you disrupting it. You'll have to leave." (That is a paraphrase.) She asked this woman out of the house, locked the door and walked away. I do not know how long she stayed there on the front porch. You say, "Well, that's not very nice." You and I need to be that way when someone comes in and tries to put their garbage in our homes. It is your sanctuary!

Do you know why people go to church? They go to church because they want hope and encouragement. If they go to church every Sunday and get beat over the head, soon they will say, "I'm not going there!" They need to go to a place where the people bless each other. They need a place where they know, "If I see her, she's going to bless me and speak well of me and she will encourage me. She's going to speak the Word over me."

You should never make plans to go into another person's sanctuary and speak evil of them, their children, or anyone else for that matter. Do not do that. That is their place of refuge. Everyone needs and deserves a place of refuge. The sad part, like I said earlier, is that the refuge for a lot of people is the local pub. It should not be.

Another thing you and I need to know is where our children are spending the night. You, as parents, are responsible for your children, and if you let them stay in a disrupted sanctuary, they pick up those things. They will bring that back into your home.

Their Own Company

Now when they saw the boldness of Peter and John, and perceived that they were unlearned and ignorant men, they marvelled; and they took knowledge of them, that they had been with Jesus. And beholding the man which was healed standing with them, they could say nothing against it. But when they had commanded them to go aside out of the council, they conferred among themselves, Saying, What shall we do to these men? for that indeed a notable miracle hath been done by them is manifest to all them that dwell in Jerusalem; and we cannot deny it. But that it spread no further among the people, let us straitly threaten them, that they speak henceforth to no man in this name. And they called them, and commanded them not to speak at all nor teach in the name of Jesus. But Peter and John answered and said unto them, Whether it be right in the sight of God to hearken unto you more than unto God, judge ye. For we cannot but speak the things which we have seen and heard. So when they had further threatened them, they let them go, finding nothing how they might punish them, because of the people: for all men glorified God for that which was done. For the man was above forty years old, on whom this miracle of healing was shewed. And being let go, they went to their own company, and reported all that the chief priests and elders had said unto them.

Acts 4:13–24 (KJV)

Now notice verse 23, "And being let go, they went to their own company, and reported all that the chief priests and elders had said unto them."

Notice that they went to their own company. Your church and your home are your sanctuary, your own company. We need to be of one mind, one voice there. Great things happen when we become of one mind and one voice!

Throughout the week you have difficult situations happen to you. Your church family may be the only family you truly have. They may be closer to you than your real family.

If the church is our sanctuary, we need to bless each other with our words. You have come to a refuge, to a place of security, a place of peace, a place where someone loves you, "Where everyone knows your name."

Go to the Complaint Department

You may be saying, "Pastor, if every man's home is their sanctuary and I cannot complain in theirs, where am I supposed to go to complain?"

It would be good if you did not have to complain, but if you cannot do that, God has a place. God has a "complaint department." You know where it is? It is in your bedchamber. It is in His presence. It is on your face before Him. Tell Him everything that you have wanted to tell everyone else. It will cause you to be blessed.

"How will that cause me to be blessed?" Your heart will change when you get into the presence of God. When your heart changes, those offenses begin to drop off and they won't matter anymore.

Our sanctuary is disrupted because of offenses. The home is our sanctuary. Some people love to go home, hide from everyone, and rest there. They are enjoying their sanctuary.

They do not want you or me to come into their home and complain. We are not supposed to do that. There is a place for that and it is called your bedchamber. God has an open ear. God wants to take care of it.

Those with an Honest Report

> And in those days, when the number of the disciples was multiplied, there arose a murmuring of the Grecians against the Hebrews, because their widows were neglected in the daily ministration. Then the twelve called the multitude of the disciples unto them, and said, It is not reason that we should leave the word of God, and serve tables. Wherefore, brethren, look ye out among you for seven men of honest report, full of the Holy Ghost and wisdom, whom we may appoint over this business.
>
> Acts 6:1–3 (KJV)

Verse 3 says, "look among you for seven men of honest report, full of the Holy Ghost." We want to ask, "Are you full of the Holy Ghost? Are you spiritual?" However, did you know "spiritual people" are not exempt from offenses?

What you look for first is a man of honest report, and then full of the Holy Ghost. A man of honest report is a person of integrity.

The word "honest" means "valuable." A man of honest or valuable report is one who has lived a practical life-style of integrity in and out of the church. They are the same in the church as they are out of the church.

The term "honest report" refers to those who have taken time to establish character. A man who has received the Holy

Spirit and a man of integrity may be two different things. The man of honest report has a firm foundation and is valuable to everyone around him.

THE KINGDOM OF GOD WITHIN YOU

We are going to highlight some of the areas we have been teaching on and show how this actually works.

What is Affecting You?

You need to understand that there is a natural system and a spiritual system. The realm of the spirit is greater, and governs everything in the natural.

We are in this natural earth, walking, living, breathing, doing business, and developing relationships. If we are not careful, when an offense happens, the flesh will get extremely angry and will take it out on others.

We have said, "Sticks and stones will break my bones, but words will never hurt me." What a lie!

Some would say, "Oh, I can handle those things. Go ahead and curse me!" If you get about 500 people cursing you, you cannot handle it. Some people cannot handle one.

I do not mean only four-letter words. Remember the word "cursing" simply means, "speaking evil of another person." Whenever you speak evil of another person, you are affecting the realm of the spirit, and the realm of the spirit affects the realm of the natural. We need to know speaking evil of another person affects a lot of people.

You may think, "I'm so insignificant that I'm not going to affect anyone or anything." Listen, what you do and what you say affects people's lives. When you speak those things out of your mouth, you may think, "That's not affecting anyone," but it is affecting someone. The number one person it is affecting is you!

We need to understand that there are two kingdoms affecting people. There is the kingdom of light and the kingdom of darkness. The things we say determine whether we are cooperating with the kingdom of light or the kingdom of darkness.

Two Kingdoms

> And he said unto them, He that hath ears to hear, let him hear. And when he was alone, they that were about him with the twelve asked of him the parable. And he said unto them, Unto you it is given to know the mystery of the kingdom of God: but unto them that are without, all these things are done in parables.
>
> Mark 4:9–11 (KJV)

In the Greek, verse 9 reads, "He that has ears to hear, let him keep on hearing." Verse 11 says, "…Unto you it is given to know the mystery of the kingdom of God…" The phrase "given to know" simply means "by experience, or intimate knowledge." So verse II can read this way, "Unto you it is given to know [by intimate knowledge] the mystery [the hidden things] of the kingdom of God: but unto them that are without, all these things are done in parables."

God has what we call the kingdom of heaven. That refers to your eternal life. As you accept Jesus as your Lord and personal Savior, you enter into the kingdom of heaven. As long as you are still here in this earth, you are walking in the kingdom of God. The kingdom of God is within us and this makes the mind of Christ available to us.

Look at Mark 4:II (KJV) again, "Unto you it is given to know the mystery of the kingdom of God..." Once you are born again, you enter into the kingdom of heaven. Your name is written in the Lamb's book of life, but as long as you are here functioning in this earth, you are in the kingdom of God.

Living Successfully

What we need to have is the manifested mind of Christ. We need to know and understand the principles of His Word and cause that Word to be manifested out of our daily lives.

The Word, or the principles of the kingdom of God, enables you to live successfully. The words spoken from your mouth cause you to become successful or cause you to fail. Whether you fail or succeeed depends upon what you do with the principles that God has already established. God does not have to re-establish His principles of success. All you have to do is to decide what you are going to do about what He has already established.

If I offend someone, I am hindering his or her walk in the kingdom of God. If you can be offended, you are hindering your walk with God. You are responsible for what you do with your life. I am respondsible for what I do with my life. If I take an offense, it is hurting me and will eventually contaminate others. If you take an offense, it is hurting you and will eventually contaminate others.

Developing Character

It is through considering these things that we develop character. If you take an offense, you have not dealt with the character issues yet. Character issues and development of character are only productive in the life of the people who are not offended. An offense stops the flow so they cannot even begin to fine-tune their character.

Taking an offense is a choice. No one makes you take an offense. You either decide to take an offense, or you decide not to. If you recall, in another chapter we read Col Stringer's article entitled, "Get Your Hand Out Of The Cage, Monkey!" that refers to a bait-stick. You will not fine-tune your character if you continue to hold onto the bait-stick.

"It's my offense. I'm going to do what I please with it." Let me tell you what will happen. The devil will steal from you. He will offer you sickness and disease, and because you are confused, you will take it. You might say, "I would never do that!"

Listen to me carefully. You do not know what you will do if you take an offense. Remember, an offense spreads into a root of bitterness. Sometimes we take an offense at the way our mother or father raised us or how they did not raise us.

We think, "It doesn't affect me," but it really does. There are times we say, "I know the Word of God. I speak the Word of God." Yet, we have that little hidden offense that is still there. It eats at us day in and day out.

Offenses do not keep you out of heaven, but they may get you there quicker. You may say, "What? Offenses can't kill you." Or can they?

Character Provides Stability

John 10:10 (KJV) tells us, "The thief cometh not, but for to steal, and to kill, and to destroy: I am come that they might have life, and that they might have it more abundantly." The word "life" used in this verse is simply referring to eternal life. The phrase "more abundantly" is referring to living fully in the kingdom of God and being successful in our daily lives.

Why is it important that you bless a child? Blessing a child is like priming a pump. As we speak blessings over him, the life of God inside of him is going to begin to be released.

If you ever curse a child, you are suppressing the life of God from ever coming to its full potential. Parents listen. I am going to tell you something practical. You may need to call your child and tell him, "I'm sorry." Your apology may set him free from offenses he's holding onto.

John 6:63 (KJV) says, "It is the spirit that quickeneth; the flesh profiteth nothing: the words that I speak unto you, they are Spirit, and they are life." Your words are spirit words, and they can speak forth death or they can speak forth life. I am talking about your words.

Matthew 12:34 (KJV) tells us, "for out of the abundance

of the heart the mouth speaketh." What is inside of you will eventually come out. Not only you will know it but also those around you will know it. If an offense is in the heart you will know it because it will produce that out of your lips. It will speak evil of other people.

Nip It in the Bud!

Barney Fife says, *"Nip it in the bud."* When you nip an offense in the bud, that means kill it right then. Then those words of cursing are not going to come out. Blessing will come out. Why? You have made a choice for blessing to come out.

We all like the excitement and ministry that goes on in the local church. We might call it the frosting on the cake. Nevertheless, the frosting is always on top of something. The foundation needs to be stable. The foundation is the stability of the whole. There are many people who never get hold of the Word. They never develop character. Character causes you to speak words that bring favor. Character is the foundation.

We are going to demonstrate how your words can be effective and how an offense that you have taken can eat away at the foundation of your life. Notice how this works.

First, you take an offense. Second, it produces a root of bitterness. Third, wrath, cursing, and speaking evil of others begins to come out of your mouth. Remember, words are spirit. Fourth, unforgiveness settles in and becomes a part of your life. Fifth, you become depressed. Sixth, you affect the production of the kingdom of God in your own personal life. Finally, a spirit of death follows you. A spirit of death represents poverty, sadness, sickness, confusion, physical death, a lack of mercy, criticism or anger, etc.

You become depressed when you take in an offense and you do not deal with it properly, and then begin to speak death. Words of death hang over your head whenever you speak out cursing of other people. We are talking about the realm of the spirit. Words affect you.

When we are talking about the spirit of death attaching itself to you, we are talking about embracing the sins of other people. If you fail to forgive them, the very same thing that is happening to them is going to happen to you.

Acting on the Truth

Some people want the truth but some people do not. They say, "Don't tell me the truth. I don't want to hear it! They are busy being offended and can't see beyond the offense. They have made everything about them.

When you have taken on an offense, you get rid of it by saying, "Father, I repent. I ask you to forgive me, and I ask you to cleanse me of all unrighteousness."

Matthew 3:8 (KJV) says there will be a fruit of forgiveness. "Bring forth therefore fruits meet for repentance." Over a period of time the seed of repentance will produce fruit.

A lot of times the words, "I'm sorry" are mouthed but they have no fruit to back them up. You may say, "I've repented of that." Time will tell. Let us watch for the fruit. The fruit is not going to lie. If you planted apples, apples are going to grow. If you plant peaches, they will come up. If you did not, they are not going to come up. If you plant offenses, they are going to grow. If you plant blessings, blessings are going to grow.

THE BOTTOM LINE

In this book about offenses we have looked at several things. We have said that offenses produce a root of bitterness, and a root of bitterness produces unforgiveness. Unforgiveness can produce hatred.

We might want to believe Spirit-filled people do not hate. However, I think it is possible that the root of bitterness, deep on the inside of you, can produce unforgiveness to such a degree that you can hate.

I am not saying it is the right thing to do. I am simply saying that there are things that go on in people's lives we do not know about. We can judge and say, "They should not do that!" Yet the reality of this is that until we have walked in that person's shoes, we are not qualified to judge them.

It is common sense that there are some things we should not do. Sometimes we do things even when we know we shouldn't. We do those things because of the situations (circumstances and people problems) we face. They cause things to happen on the inside of us.

The situations that occurred with some television ministers created some problems in the body of Christ. There have been a lot of people, Christian and non-Christian alike, judging those men. I am convinced beyond a shadow of a doubt that none of those ministers started out intending to do any of the things they ended up doing.

The reason we have looked at these situations with magnifying glasses is because those ministers were ordained to be holy and right, and all of a sudden they were not. We need to look and see why it happened.

I am not going to tell you I have the answer to their situation, or to yours. I am simply saying there is a common thread that seems to run through the body of Christ that is important.

Some people have been very good at taking the road of offenses to their own demise. Little by little the offenses begin to cause death to overtake their lives. That death, in the form of bitterness, turns into wrath. Wrath turns into hate, and hate produces death.

The Ability to Forget

In Isaiah 43:25 (KJV) we read that, "I, even I, am he that blotteth out thy transgressions for mine own sake, and will not remember thy sins." Why does God do that? We think God does whatever He wants to do. However, He will not act beyond His Word. If God's Word says it, that is what He will do. That is His integrity. Those are His guidelines, and He will not fail.

God will not violate His Word. This is the integrity of His Word. He will not go beyond His Word. His Word is His boundary. He wants you and I to have the same type of integrity.

If we make a statement we need to honor it. That is our integrity. God will honor His Word that we speak. He says, "I, even I, am he that blotteth out thy transgressions for mine own sake, and will not remember thy sins." The reason God has done that is because it is His Word that He spoke out of His mouth. It is a universal law; He doesn't go back on His word; what He speaks comes to pass.

Not only will He forgive but He also forgets. God said, "Not only do I forgive, but, also, I will not remember your sins any further." (see Isaiah 43:25)

That is like someone who said to the Father, "I have missed it here, I have done this. Will you forgive me?" He forgives in a heartbeat.

The devil comes immediately and says, "You can't expect forgiveness." So that person runs back to the altar and says, "God, I asked you to forgive me. Would you forgive me?" And God says, "What are you talking about?"

His Word says that He remembers those sins no more. That means He forgets them. Wouldn't you like to be able to forget some things that happened to you in the past?

Things that happen to us alter our life-style, our thinking, and what we believe and do. People tend to believe their experiences instead of the Word of God. Our experiences are thieves and robbers. We need to begin to work on forgetting those things and start looking at the Word.

Can You Forgive and Forget?

Can you and I forgive and forget? I believe that we can. I am not suggesting that you and I are like God and can forgive and forget just like that. However, there is a place in God where you can hide and dwell under the shadow of the Almighty, and the past actually becomes difficult to recall. If we continually rehearse the past it is easy to recall. The Hebrew word for remember is translated "remention." As we remention the past, we continue to remember it.

If we say, "I forgive you, but I'm not going to forget," have we really forgiven? More than likely we have not forgiven completely.

I knew of a devastating situation in a man's life and I thought, "He will learn from that." But he took forgiveness to an extreme and went right back into that situation. I asked him why he was back in that same situation and he said, "Well, I forgave them, and if I truly forgave them, that means that I should go back to the situation." I said, "Wait a minute. Don't do that."

Do not make forgiveness mean something that it does not mean. When you forgive that person, bless them instead of cursing them, but do not put yourself in the same mess again. Make a quality decision to forgive.

Do not only forgive that person but also work on forgetting this situation. *You can forget the hurt of a situation without forgetting the wisdom of not letting it happen again.* The ability to forget needs to be worked into these areas of offenses.

> Brethren, I count not myself to have apprehended: but this one thing I do, forgetting those things which are behind, and reaching forth unto those things which are

before, I press toward the mark for the prize of the high
calling of God in Christ Jesus. Let us therefore, as many
as be perfect, be thus minded: and if in anything ye be
otherwise minded, God shall reveal even this unto you.

Philippians 3:13–15, KJV

If your heart is toward God and you truly seek God concerning the past, the present, and even the future, He says that
He will reveal it to you.

A Matter of Integrity

When things do not go right, people often begin to look for
someone else to blame. There may have been some things
that happened to create the problem but you do not need to
look outside yourself. You need to look inside. We need to
examine our hearts to see what we are doing.

Granted, things may have happened in situations so they
are not what you would like for them to be. However, true
success is not based on what happens in the world. True success is based on what happens inside of you. How do you
handle what is going on in there?

If you are not dealing with what is going on in your soul,
you are just fooling yourself. You will lose even the appear-
ance of success.

I read an article about one man who worked in a manu-
facturing company. His son got to the age where he decided
his parents did not know anything. "Dad's just an old hillbilly,"
he said. The father had been working in the same factory for
many years, but the son decided he was not going to do that.

His dad had already told him that integrity and doing

things the right way would always pay off. But the son ignored what his dad said, went off to college, and then got a job with an advertising company.

The son conducted his business with the idea that it is all right to do whatever you need to do to get the sale, and worry about what it produces later. The son had no integrity, and that was the way he ran his business. For a while he made a lot of money.

However, one day the boss called and said to him, "I need to have a very important meeting with you in the morning before everybody gets here." The young man thought he must have made a big sale because he was the only one being called in to discuss it.

He got there early and the boss told him, "Because of your lack of integrity, I do not have any more work for you. I want you out of here before 8 o'clock."

The young man was crushed, and the first place he went was to his dad. He and his dad started talking about things. Finally, the young man began to see that success is not "flash." Success involves stability and integrity. He had to forget the past, look to the future, and start again.

The bottom line is that we must have integrity. Forgiveness is necessary in order to have integrity. Success is established only to the degree to which you have forgiven and released people, forgotten the past and reached forward to the future.

Running the Race

Brethren I count not myself to have apprehended: but this one thing I do, forgetting those things, which are behind, and reaching forth unto those things which are

before. I press toward the mark for the prize of the high
calling of God in Christ Jesus. [or I press toward those
things that are before me.]

Philippians 3:13, 14

The word "forgetting" in the Greek means "completely forgetting." It is making reference to a runner running a race. If
I am running a race, my concentration on the other runners
affects my ability to win the race. As long as I am recalling
the past, or that which is behind me, it slows me down in
what I want to accomplish.

You may think, "I don't know if I can do that! How can I
forget what they did to me?" I am not going to tell you that
it is easy. However, I believe that there is a place in God that
you can forget the past, and go forward.

In order to forget the past you have to make a quality decision to forgive. If you do not forgive you are not going to forget. The past will be a noose around your neck. What is past
has already happened. What are you going to do about it?

Some people hold onto what has happened in the past to
such a degree that they are not able to run any more races. If
they are running a race, they will look and see if the past is still
there. The more they look back, the slower they go and they will
take fewer strides forward. Philippians 3:13 (KJV) says, "But this
one thing I do, forgetting those things which are behind, and
reaching forth unto those things which are before."

All of us have made mistakes and suffered hurts and
offenses. However, a sad indictment to us and to the body of
Christ is that we still make mistakes because we have not for-

gotten or forgiven those things. We will end up making worse mistakes because of the baggage we are dragging with us.

Free from the Past

Remember the illustration that we presented earlier about the demonic spirit that was chained to me because of offenses? I had to tell him, "Unchain me! Turn loose of me!" If I could have looked into the realm of the Spirit, I would have seen that ugly thing chained to me. You do not want that demonic spirit involved in everything you do! And, yet at the expense of their total success, some people fail to forgive. They dwell on the past, and nothing happens!

Here are four things we need to pay attention to so that we can forget the past.

> And be found in him, not having mine own righteousness, which is of the law, but that which is through the faith of Christ, the righteousness which is of God by faith: That I may know him, and the power of his resurrection, and the fellowship of his sufferings, being made conformable unto his death; If by any means I might attain unto the resurrection of the dead....Let us therefore, as many as be perfect, be thus minded: and if in any thing ye be otherwise minded, God shall reveal even this to you.
>
> Philippians 3:9–11,15 (KJV)

Found in Him

The first is found in verse 9, "and be found in him." Unless you and I know who we are in Christ there is going to be a lot of flesh hanging around. We need to know and understand who we are "in Him." Your strongest desire needs to be that others see Jesus in you. We say, "All I want is for people to see Jesus in me." We make that statement, and it sounds good, but if our next thought is to remember how someone wronged us, no one will see Christ in us. What we are holding against others is what they will see.

Matthew 5:16 (KJV) says to, "Let your light so shine before men, that they may see your good works, and glorify your Father which is in heaven." Do you know what most Christians have to do? They have to make their light shine. There is a difference in letting your light shine and making your light shine.

If you turn the lights off for just a moment and then turn them on again, the lights do not groan and strain to try to come on. They are made to shine. That is just what they do.

You and I can walk in the presence of God to the point that, even when we get into a tough situation, we will not have to force our light to shine; it will automatically shine. However, if you and I are carrying baggage from offenses and trying to collect debts, we have to make it shine. We have to say the right thing at the right time. When you and I get lost in Him we do not have to make anything happen—it just happens.

Knowing Him

The second thing we must pay attention to in order to forget is the phrase, "That I may know Him." The Greek used here for the word "know" means "to know by experience, or to come to know by experience." When I am saying, "to know Him" I am talking about getting into His presence.

I believe the Word points this out. The two ingredients to maturity are the Spirit and the Word. There are a lot of Word people who do not want anything to do with the Spirit. They say, "I will just teach the Word!" Yes, we need to teach the Word. But I have found that if all we are doing is teaching the Word and we fail to allow the Spirit to work, we are not really growing in maturity.

Then there are those who have a hard time receiving teaching and prefer an emotional service; but the retention of the Word is what changes our hearts. It takes the Spirit and the Word to cause us to grow up into maturity and in the things of God. He is saying here, "to know Him." Getting into the presence of God involves our prayer time. To know the Word involves our devotional time.

When we get into the presence of God, His presence begins to become a part of us. We have said the confession of the Word out of our mouth changes our circumstances. It is our time spent in His presence that changes us.

True maturity is staying in the presence of God and letting Him be the ingredient that causes our hearts to be soft and pliable instead of hardened. What hardens a person's heart? One thing is unforgiveness. When your heart is hardened, God has a difficult time getting in and causing you to succeed.

The Power of His Resurrection

The third thing we need to pay attention to so we can forget is "the power of His resurrection" (Philippians 3:10, KJV).

We can experience the same power surging through our own being that raised Christ from the dead.

Romans 8:11 (KJV) says, "if the Spirit of him that raised up Jesus from the dead dwell in you," or in your body. The power that raised Jesus from the dead resides on the inside of your temple!

The Fellowship of His Sufferings

Finally, the fourth thing we need to pay attention to so we can forget is: "the fellowship of his sufferings, being made comformable unto his death." (Philippians 3:10, KJV)

The Greek language used in this verse indicates a "joint participation." Many people have misunderstood the sufferings he's talking about here. People have said, "Well, I am just suffering for Jesus with this physical affliction." No, you are not suffering for Jesus with that affliction. Jesus paid for that. Matthew 5:10–12 shows our joint participation with God.

> Blessed are they which are persecuted for righteousness' sake: for theirs is the kingdom of heaven. Blessed are ye, when men shall revile you, and persecute you, and shall say all manner of evil against you falsely, for my sake. Rejoice, and be exceeding glad: for great is your reward in heaven: for so persecuted they the prophets which were before you.
>
> Matthew 5:10–12 (KJV)

Once the life of God begins to be made manifest in you, there are going to be people who will persecute you. He says that if they are persecuting you for righteousness sake, rejoice! If they are saying all manner of evil against you falsely, rejoice.

So many Christians think suffering is referring to physical suffering. One time I helped a man apply for acceptance into a ministry. He asked me to fill out a reference for him. Afterward, I received their statement of faith which required them to take a vow of poverty. Take a vow of poverty! We think we don't believe that, but some people accept a vow of poverty mentally, and say, "I am just suffering for Jesus." Listen, what does the Word say about Jesus, becoming "poor, that ye through his poverty might be rich"? (2 Corinthians 8:9, KJV)

"Joint participation" simply means that we are conforming to the image of the one who redeemed us. We are talking about the ability to forget. The closer you conform to the image of the Lord Jesus Christ on the inside of you, the more you will find that your heart is after that one thing - "I don't care about anything else other than Jesus being in me."

Why Forget?

We have talked about how to forget, but we also need to understand why we need to forget.

There is a place in God where we can, "press toward the mark of the prize of the high calling of God in Christ Jesus," to the extent that we realize we have forgotten those things that have happened before.

You need to forget the past. It is a dead weight that will hold you down. You must want Jesus so much that everything else fades away. Paul said, in Philippians 3:8 (KJV), "… and do count them but dung…" or "I count all things but loss."

Anytime we begin to bring up our past, or walk under the law, we are thinking that God is saying, "Well, you did this so there is a consequence. This is what I am going to require of you...." No, God's grace is there to help you, but we have not accepted it. Unless we accept God's grace, we are going to end up doing some things on our own, and it will cost us.

I honestly believe you and I can forget. We have to be willing to. Once you have forgiven, then make it a priority and say, "Not only have I forgiven, but I am going to put this thing so far behind me that I am going to forget it. I am going to hide my life in the Lord Jesus Christ." Psalms 91:1 says, "He that dwelleth in the secret place of the most high..." We are to make that our abode. God is there and His arms are open to us. When people come against us, we should run into the cleft of the Rock. He encloses us with His arms.

In His presence nothing else matters. You will not even know that anything else is going on.

John 4:24 (KJV) talks about, "they that worship Him." The word "worship" in the Greek is *proskineo* which means "face to face." Whenever you come face to face with God the Father Himself, you will change!

Are you having problems forgetting what happened in the past? The real problem is not that you cannot forget. The problem is you have not spent enough time in the presence of God! When we go there, He speaks His deep things to our heart.

Have you been offended? That offense is a seed that Satan can use to destroy you. The seed of offense will produce a root of bitterness, which in turn produces wrath, which finally produces unforgiveness. Unforgiveness has no limits to its destructive force.

The only place you can get rid of unforgiveness is in the presence of God. Run to Jesus, not away from Him.